CUSTOMER'S ADVISORY:

Conceptualization, Definition and Explanation

Mustafa Özgür Güngör

2009

...TO MY BELOVED FAMILY

TABLE OF CONTENTS

1   INTRODUCTION

In today's globally competitive market, organizations are in need of cultivating an enhanced customer-centric culture. By strategically using customer feedback, the organizations are able to improve interactions across all possible customer touch points, extend customer relationship and lifetime value through better communication and become able to guide product innovation to match emerging market values and demand, so as to assure long term market existence and profitability.

The prolonged, traditional understanding of production in organizations was symbolized as a group of interacting processes which take inputs as resources and efficiently turn them into outputs as products. Following product-oriented and sales-oriented eras, this mechanical model was seriously challenged by the focus in market-orientation for competition (Shapiro, 1988; Kohli and Jaworski, 1990; Slater and Narver, 1994; Ruekert, 1992; Day, 1999). Later, the threat is amplified by the perfection in production systems and the ease of imitation besides the increasing number of global marketing challenges (Stephens, 1996). One of the forthcoming ideas to eliminate these kinds of threats is assuring differentiation by focusing on the involvement of customers.

From the organizational point of view, the process of "customer acquisition" (Ang and Buttle, 2006) in competitive consumer markets necessitates satisfaction of higher value expectations set by the consumer community (Voss and Voss, 2008). It also encompasses delving into higher barriers built by many competitors through increasing number of additional services provided. The consumer is getting more mobile and interactive by each technological advance. It gets harder to be recognized and remembered among messages the buyer is exposed so that it becomes more important to stay upfront in consumer's mind.

Therefore, organizations are forced to become sophisticated organisms rather than mechanical allies. As organizations are in need to reinvent better ways to execute their core businesses, they realize that it is becoming harder to stay competitive if innovativeness is not incubated into the organizational culture. Although this idea is affirmative, giving way to creative mindset, innovative thinking and evaluation capability within an existing system are the most prominent internal drivers for organizations. They are supposed to be well connected with their surroundings like the supplier network and customer community. Ideally, the organizations are moving in the direction of superiority by turning their relationships with "actors" (customers, employees, partners, and suppliers) in their environment into an essential part of product and service innovation and evaluation.

A very basic part of these relations is the request of organization for customer involvement. Some important aspects of service evaluation capability for organizations are: skills and talents within the organization, knowledgeable resources to be attainable, being able to learn easily and the ability to attach meaning to overcome complicated puzzles of business life. Hence to cope with both consumer market dynamics and changes in competition factors via innovativeness, requires a new perspective to "consumer behavior" to retain advantage from its kinetics thorough understanding of a new approach, namely the "customer's advisory" in the field of marketing.

1.1 The Struggle of Organizations

Turkish organizations face three main challenges to remain competitive: In the local markets there is the growing competition stimulated by the domestic firms on the one side, and the international competitors widening their market environments in a variety of ways on the other. In markets abroad they face other challenges of competition such as the requirement to understand market dynamics to be able to respond in time. These challenges were existent for a long time but they became more apparent as the globalization fostered them. Firms which are up to date, following the needs and requirements in the market and adapting themselves to these changes seem to respond better to challenging situations and remain competitive. This in a way reflects their focus on a modernist approach. Therefore, for a better understanding of this situation it is good to drill into how a contemporary organization is constituted.

From a general perspective, an organization focuses on three conceptual dimensions (Figure 1.1):

- organizational development

- customer development

- service development

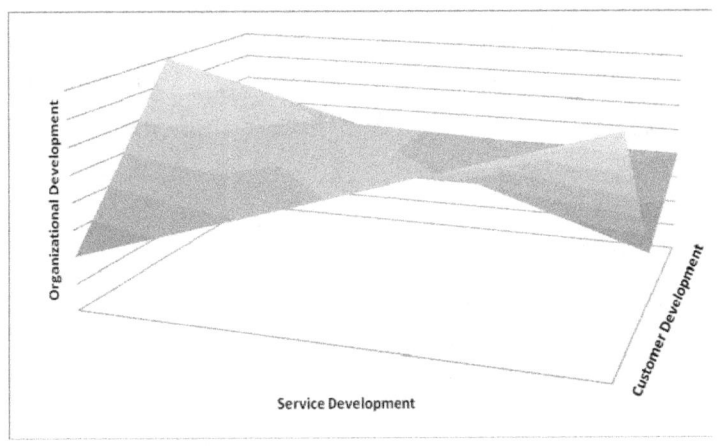

Figure 1.1 Three focus dimensions of modern
organization

The first one, based on the ideas of Lusch and Vargo
(2004), is represented by the foundations of service
dominant logic of marketing (SDLM) as: "the composition
of service". Service is not a static mean of proposition by
the activities of organization but it includes the value co-
created with the customer and inherits the knowledge in
previous experiences of organization. These include
increasing product, quality (Jacobson and Aaker, 1987)
and service quality (Carman, 1990; Babakuş and Boller,
1992; Cronin and Taylor 1994; Buttle, 1996; Zeithaml et
al., 1996; Parasuraman et al, 1985, 1988, 1991b and
1994, Chenet et. al, 1999), learning about consumer

decision-making, and sustainability in the life of customer relationships (Morgan and Hunt, 1994; Koslowsky, 2001). In Figure 1.1, this first dimension is named as "*service development*".

The second one is related with organizational behavior. An organization is not a solitude monolithic construction, anymore. It has capabilities of learning and changing (Levitt and March, 1988; Senge, 1990), adaptation and expansion (Hammer and Champy, 1993), and collapsing or revolving (Gibson, 1996). These abilities are making a dynamic nature available for organizational development. Many studies (Gummesson, 2002; Parasuraman and Grewal, 2000b; Cooper, 2000; Walker and Ruekert, 1987) cover the analysis of managerial strategies and organizational dynamics, all of which symbolized as "*organizational development*" in Figure 1.1.

The third aspect, which is one of the foremost discussion matters of the last several decades, can be defined as "*customer development*". Customer development includes increasing the number of customers and their interactions with the organization by providing consistent and sustainable, all-round integrated messages as well as comprehensive support of the services. As Gobé (2002)

10

pointed out, "...the true dynamic to trust [between organization and customer] is based on a continuous, reciprocal 'give and take' principle that recognizes the very powerful, active role of the consumer on a continual basis" (p.47).

Porter (2008) underlines this issue from competition and value interrelationship point of view and he addresses an important opportunity of differences in customer strategies affective on superior performance: "...differences in customers, suppliers, substitutes, potential entrants, and rivals that can become the basis for distinct strategies yielding superior performance. In a world of more open competition and relentless change, it is more important than ever to think structurally about competition" (p.14).

Every modern organization, like an organism, has a momentum of evolution in these dimensions over time axis by the effects of environmental forces, competition factors, and changing customer expectations. For each dimension of the modern organization there is enforcement for permanent dynamic structuring to remain and surge benefits from the competitive markets. In Figure 1.2, the organization's status for that moment

11

in the time axis is represented with different shapes. This iteration symbolizes that any dimension would be relatively high or low in accordance to the changes in the market, consumer expectations, advancements or failures in any organizational operation.

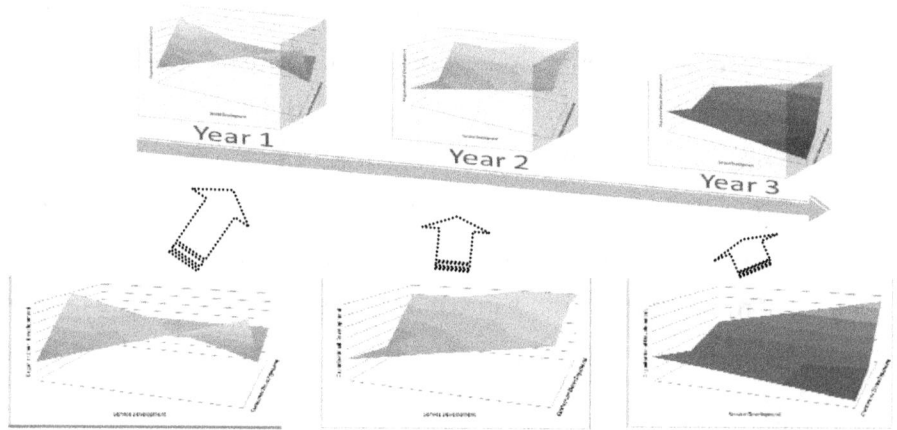

Figure 1.2 Three dimensions of modern organization with time axis

1.2 Customer's Advisory as a Driver of Innovation

Customers are affected daily by thousands of messages (Fisk, 2006; Tek 2006) and their attitudes are reshaped in accordance to many sublime impulses (Zaltman, 2003). On the other hand, almost every market-oriented organization is able to collect data about dynamics of customer behavior. Nevertheless, just by the collection of similar information from the markets, a detailed analysis of fundamental strategic capabilities of the firm leaves lesser space to maneuver for differentiation.

As a matter of fact, it is getting more critical to derive insights from the responses of the customers by placing them right in the core. Organizations are adapting themselves to better listening and sensing the future expectations, by relying on customer's advisory referred through all active channels.

In parallel with the challenge stated above, the technological renaissance that powered consumer in communication and decision-making also opens a new window for innovation and evaluation of products and services.

A drive of customer-orientation and relationship management movement led the organizations to set priorities to build appropriate technological advancements for communication with customers like toll-free phone lines, web sites, and call centers. However, these developments were brought by a managerial strategy of taking customer complaints into account rather than orientation of a strategy around all round satisfaction of customer. So, their outcomes were generally results of a top-down managerial design directed to customers, with the aim of informing them about the organizational side and product-service side of the organization, and listening to some extend to complaints.

But today market dynamics require rather a bottom-up approach[1]:

_____

[1] Bottom up approach in market dynamics have been rather discussed under "agent-based modelling", relevant for many

14

- listening to expectations and perceptions of customers from a new perspective to reshape and reformulate the business strategies

- (and even more) using their unconditionally given feedbacks to innovate new products and services

In a customer-oriented organization, the ultimate goal is providing superior customer value (Weinstein and Johnson, 1999) and gaining competitive advantage (Huber et. al 2001). The value can also be assured by focusing on the service failures as a learning process to avoid them in the future. In the 21st century, satisfaction of higher expectations of customers is based on detailed focus of customer contacts, customer data, and relationships with the organization. In parallel with the requirements to meet such expectations, marketing technology tools evaluated from foundational concepts and definitions first addressed by Bartels (1965). For the last

---

scientific areas by Whitman et al. (2001), Chen and Yeh (2001), and Bonabeau (2002).

decades, marketing technology is getting more integrated into enterprise resource planning and management through business intelligence tools and covers also customer relationship management solutions, the use of the Internet on both internal and external information sharing.

Beyond listening to the customers to analyze their complaints and evaluations, it became more and more important to involve the customer into the process of marketing. The activities to support customer involvement and to capture distilled advisory are more critical processes of modern organization than before. Market driven organizations (Day, 1999) are becoming more and more customer driven. In a business to consumer market, challenged by competition factors, innovative services are accustomed to the needs of various minor segments of customers. These segments are required to be understood, very well communicated and even build by the interaction so as to serve for a better brand equity, which in turn can assure higher level of recognition to the organization. For a general abbreviation, organizations analyze the market, anticipate the needs, design, shape and provide solutions though their understanding.

Generally, their main issue is waiting for responses like complaints as a feedback to activate an innovative system. However, there are possibly more valuable comments to listen to and build into the strategy process, if the communication would be started by the customer towards the organization regarding the evaluation of the product and service. This, in brief, is called "customer's advisory".

Customer's advisory is a general term for capturing the responses and advises of customers for evaluation of products and services that the organization is offering. It requires technological focus to capture and analyze responses, it is based on responsiveness and empathy in organizational culture, and it fosters the capability of product and service evaluation. The responses and advisory of customers can be critically supportive for evaluation and innovation within the organization. In Figure 1.3, cyclic factors of innovation of Berkhout and van der Duin (2006) include two important aspects such as "society oriented science cycle" and "customized service cycle" those intrigue the issue of customer's advisory and innovation relationship. One of the most important characteristics of this model is its shape. The cyclic design indicates

17

that innovation can start in any factor in this cycle and revolves to other factors. This approach in the model underlines that implementing an innovative organizational thinking is not a subsequent chain of actions such as research and development department starts it up and customer ends. Instead, innovation in the evaluation of services could possibly be started by the customer in "customized service cycle" if the organization has the capability and openness.

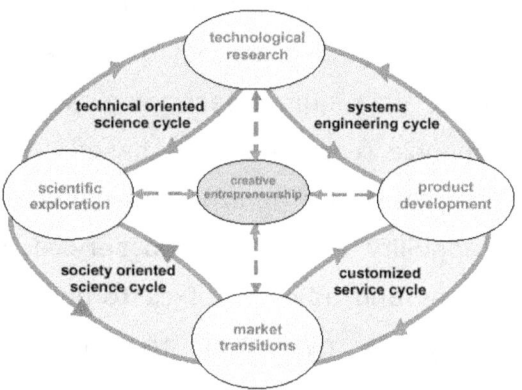

Figure 1.3 Cyclic innovation model[2]

---

[2] Berkhout and van der Duin (2006), "New ways of innovation: an application of Cyclical Innovation Model to mobile telecom industry"

In addition, Bonabeau et al. (2008) define the monolithic process of new product development for the companies as in two stages, early and late: In the early stage, where the company focused on the evaluation of prospects and elimination of "bad bets" [of product idea], as Bonabeau et al. (2008) stress, the common mistake of managers is ignoring evidences that indicate possible failure of their assumptions about a new service. In the late stage, where company tries to maximize the potentials of the candidates, the common error is termination of the project prematurely because of improper projections. Bonebeau et al. (2008) further observed such conditions in real-life examples; they address the problems belonging the process of product or service development from inside-out the organization. Still in this issue, an outside-in view from "customer's advisory" would help to overcome problems in each stage with some probability. If evaluation of prospects is backed up with "customer's advisory" then most prominent prospects would become apparent and the number of bad bets would be lesser than expected. In addition, effective interpretation of "customer's advisory" would also decrease the improbability of the projections about new product development projects.

19

These extensions in customer oriented strategies are backed up with the inventions in tools of marketing communications and have important effects in the future of marketing strategies of the organizations. From this perspective, the background of this book is based on the marketing strategy framework with a focus on relationship marketing, integrated marketing communication and consumer behavior domains. It is aimed at demystification of the impacts of this changing and improving role of the customer in the service evaluation. Assessment of the understanding of changing role of the customer is subjected to be investigated through the identification and analysis of the effects in strategic imperatives.

In this perspective, six different fundamental concepts, laws and theories are discussed briefly in compilation of the model throughout this book which addresses both of strategic imperatives. These are: resource-advantage theory (Hunt, 1997; Hunt and Arnett, 2003), relationship marketing theory (Berry, 1983; Sheth and Parvatiyar, 1995; Grönroos, 2004), integrated marketing communication (Kitchen and Schultz, 2003), service dominant logic of marketing approach (Lusch and Vargo, 2004, 2006), knowledge management (Tiwana, 2001) and brand communities (Muniz and O'Guinn, 2001). Therefore, theoretical foundation of this matter is related to the examination of three distinct advisory roles of the customer with the support of market-oriented organizations, relationship marketing, resource advantages, and service dominant approach:

- contribution to the design of service (advisor, responsive service evaluators)
- collaboration with brand community (recommender, voluntary marketers of services)
- disseminating opposition information (disliker, stoppers among consumer market)

In brief, aim of this book was conceptualized around the identification of measure and acting factors for making use of customer's advisory via marketing technology tools incorporated by Turkish organizations to evaluate or to innovate better service for the achievement of superior financial performance and superior customer value.

2 CUSTOMER-ORIENTED COMPETITIVENESS

The bold definition of converged services and products are addressed by many marketing researchers and practitioners lately. According to the new genre of customers those born in the realization of customer-oriented era, Ridderstrale and Nordström (2000) point that "Products and services are also blurring...Atoms and bits co-exist in most modern customer offerings." (p.112), while they were analyzing the new society, its fragmentation, and its "funky" nature. There is a more serious challenge regarding the changing role of customer in the definition of service, its nature and its value. Lusch and Vargo (2004) stressed that there is a new approach to understand the dynamics of customer with services of organizations and they opened up the debate to gather most of the giant thinkers of marketing science.

Payne and Frow (2005) indicated that strategic development process which was composed of business and customer strategies was found related with value creation processes, information management processes, integration and performance assessment processes of the organization. Information management part of this strategic development included technology systems and analytical tools for customer behavior, value and social interaction analysis with the organizations, namely a better configured customer relationship management system by Payne and Frow (2005).

Moreover, the role of technology, its supportive tools are also acting upon this relationship between customer and organization's offerings. The analysis of related concepts is discussed further in different sections: The evaluation and effects of customer value and customer equity; the definition and the importance of customer's advisory, the use of the technology to get customer feedback and ideas; brand communities and their amplification of interaction with the brand; and the defined strategic imperatives and their synthesis. The literature survey about these concepts is explained in the following sections.

2.1 Customer Value and Customer Equity

Gale (1994) pointed out that "customer value is the most important concept and the most important target in business management" (p.23) and in order to reach goals of profitability, growth and increased shareholder value set by the organization, exceptional customer value generation is required. In his thought provoking book "Managing Customer Value", Gale proposed a methodology to establish better customer value that depends on three major components: (1) understanding customer needs, (2) providing superior quality in areas that matter to customers, and (3) communicating effectively with customers to ground market-perceived quality. Some other supportive researches followed his pathway. One of which was the discussion of Zeithaml et al. (1996), posing the

24

relation of retention of customers at the aggregate level with service quality. They found out those behavioral intentions of customers show strong evidence of service quality perception and therefore influencing their retention. Another support was the study of Thomas et al. (2004), where the researchers explored the intersection of communication frequency, relationship duration and profitability. Their findings imply that there is a positive correlation between profitability and relationship with customer depending on duration of this relationship and effective communication.

Tek (2006) follows Gale's hypothesis and defines a comprehensive "Value Package" as the whole range of benefits that an organization proposes to present its customers in harmonization. This value package contains communication, intermediation and satisfaction components. Dynamic nature of these components is like floating messages of value proposals around consumer waiting to be selected and start a relationship. According to the same author, customer equity is a sum of net present values of customer lifetime values of all customers of organization. For this reason, customer lifetime value

25

(CLV) (Malthouse and Blattberg, 2004; Dwyer, 1997), is one of the essential keys in strategic management as it comprehends all of the elements from service quality to return on marketing investment (ROMI).

From this perspective, CLV and customer equity concepts are descriptive for better performance of organization. As Pfeifer et al. (2005) reflect, organizations prosper by learning how to capitalize on customer differences throughout the use of CLV measurement. Former approaches for calculation of CLV are discussed by Jain and Singh (2002) from various foundational aspects such as customer migration, optimal resource allocation, and customer relationship handling. Based on these, a recent model for estimating CLV has been developed by Malthouse and Blattberg (2004). One of the latest elaborations on this estimation function is completed by Gupta and Lehmann (2005) that included retention parameters, growth margins and time horizon into formulation. In this book, some effective parameters of CLV are subject to be investigated as they bring out the possibly of having implications on customer's advisory. CLV, "The present value of future cash flows attributed to customer relationship" is by definition a derivation from relationship management (Grönroos, 2004) and it is an integral argument in the evaluation of customer equity. Looking from this angle, Lemon et al. (2001) has developed a diagnostic framework of customer equity. In their work, they combine CLV, brand equity and customer behavior analysis into customer equity pot. By this way, customer equity is an ultimate valuation determinant for organization on the long-run about management of its customer-base and contemplating better marketing strategies. Lemon et al (2001) defined the three independent drivers of customer equity as value equity, brand equity, and relationship equity. This approach is supported by the brand manifold concept of Berthon et al. (2007), Tek's (2006) abbreviation of rituals belonging to the extended relationship with brand and its consumers, and backed up with Gupta and Lehmann's (2005) calculations.

According to the literature, the most prominent components for customer equity are the building units of value, brand and relationship aspects of it. Therefore, as Ruyter and Wetzels (1998), Lemon et al. (2001), and Berry and Bendapudi (2003) underline, the key leverages of value are quality, cost, and convenience; the key customer equity specific drivers of brand are awareness, attitude, and corporate ethics; and the key levers of relationship are loyalty programs, customer treatment, affinity programs, and community-building activities.

Another extension on Gale's (1994) approach, was initiated by Lusch and Vargo (2004) where they underline in the preface section (p. xvii), relating with their previous works, that "marketing is the process in society and organizations that facilitates voluntary exchange through collaborative relationships that create reciprocal value through application of complementary resources" and they impose that one of the essential elements of marketing is the emphasis of voluntary exchange and collaborative relationships. In fact, current definition of marketing by American Marketing Association (AMA) incorporates and emphasizes also value concept and moves away from the simple definition of an exchange.

In Lusch and Vargo's (2004) conceptualization of SDLM, service becomes one of the most important keys to ensemble better relationship with consumers to make customers out of them: Customer is the one who believes that the service is satisfactory and available at a value s/he can define. From this point of view, all others who do not believe in value proposition by the brand stay in the consumer pool and they demand more of just a product to become customer. They demand better service components which comprise the product. SDLM defines that the service is an aggregate product or an ultimate product and completes the benefits that product proposes.

However, as consumers are polygamists (Tek, 2006) by nature, it is fairly hard to build a long-lasting relationship with a customer unless brand moves in harmonization with the tides of psychographic matters. A customer is loosely reluctant to return back to consumer status as Dick and Basu (1994) stated, but also this loyalty schema does not imply a customer is a monogamist. Therefore, listening to market for facilitation of the customer's advisory became crucial for organizations, if they want to turn consumers into customers and keep them out from rivals. Organizations prefer committed relationships rather than one-time basis because of higher cost of acquisition investment made for a new customer. For a solution to this commitment problem, the role of customer relationship management (CRM) became important as for the controlling and evaluation the progress of creating better customer equity. Payne and Frow (2005) formulated the context of CRM as "a strategic approach that is concerned with creating improved shareholder value through the development of appropriate relationships with key customers and customer segments..." (p.168); hence CRM is an essential marketing technology tool for enabling relationship assets. Admitting that customers and relationships are assets, the management of this asset is required. CRM, if properly configured with truly customer-centric mindset, supports acquisition of new customers from consumer mass, enhances the value of existing customers, retains profitable customers, maximizes customer profitability, and supports customer satisfaction. It enables customer life-cycle analysis, CLV measurement, customer profitability measurement, and better business intelligence.

As a final discussion for this section, the sum of interrelation between CLV, SDLM and CRM can be reflected as follows: an advising customer is a more valuable asset. The capability of organization to capture customer's advisory and reading between the lines of this commentary, and to put it back into the production system in plain and neatly explained way is critically important. As a result of collecting such data, an analysis by "imperatives" upon dimensions discussed in Figure 1.1 is becoming possible. By this way, reengineering these commentaries to design new features, to elaborate services and to refurbish existing products is a lot easier. This process as a whole is the key to build new marketing strategies optimized for the organization. These customer's advisory based strategies would flatter various affects on the units of organization for: benchmarking, product development, complaint management, as well as managerial-operational strategy evaluation.

2.2 Customer's Advisory and the Use of Technology

Customer's advisory is a result of modern approach in organizations (in Figure 1.1 and Figure 1.2) and it is an intersecting area of three dimensions, namely service, organizational and customer development. It is one of the most influential dominating factors of development where customer plays the leading role.

There is a momentum of dynamism in customer's interpretation of alternatives. Thus, is dependent on the factors of irrationality, subconscious affections and intimate decision-making (Zaltman, 2003), but mostly is effected by gravity of its social networks. Therefore, if the organization is listening to the responses and customer's advisory properly, it fosters a great potential to develop new or elaborated, better functionalizing, customized, and direct service for its markets. Organizations are on the verge of implementing tools of one-to-one social ties with their customers through tools such as integrated emailing, chat servers, blogs, digs, social networking sites, commentaries, and forums. These tools let marketing communication became a comprehensive way of dialogue for listening to the responses and comments, capturing ideas and depicting the requirements for new features in product and service; named as "customer's advisory". According to American Marketing Association, the list of marketing hot topics includes seven items where five of them are directly related with globalization and marketing technologies: CRM, Competitive Affairs, Global Marketing, Integration of Sales and Marketing, Multicultural Marketing.

Dedication to customer-oriented service is supported by some of the "interlocked enablers" which show the trend in behavioral dynamics of consumers for the last decades. These were emerging from the effects of globalization and "technological renaissance", where consumers reached a higher level of communication with every other party. A prominent collection of these enablers are presented below in a general chronological order:

- Customer loyalty became a critical element in the competition. (Reichheld, 1996)
- Consumer-rights are getting more important than in previous decades and some of the basic legal amendments are already completed in favor of defending customers against abuse.
- Consumer consciousness increased. Consumers are more interested in the ingredients of products as well as environmentally friendly and ethical production and marketing activities (Borak, 1995). In addition, the Internet is getting wider user base. Many new web sites provide a good medium to be informed about the product and service details as well as for a better comparison of the alternatives in the market.

- Consumer behavior is changing in the direction of becoming more post-modern (Fırat et al, 1995; Christensen et al, 2005): dynamic, self-confident, variant, open, and compromising.

- Developments in technology initiated three interrelated levels of foundation: database infrastructure and user-friendliness for data storage (database management is easier than last decades and it is becoming widely used by early users of Microsoft Excel to more complicated ones), the Internet infrastructure and the web interfaces for data collection (even bloggers can save content-data online without interference of any technical assistance), wireless networking infrastructure (from Bluetooth[3], and WiMax[4] to 3G[5] and CDMA[6]) and

---

[3] Definition by www.bluetooth.org special interest group and Wikipedia (www.wikipedia.com): "Bluetooth is a wireless protocol utilizing short-range communications technology facilitating data transmission over short distances from fixed and mobile devices, creating wireless personal area networks."

[4] WiMax Forum (www.wimaxforum.org) defines WiMax as "WiMAX is a standards-based technology enabling the delivery of last mile

mobile devices for data interactivity at large (increasing number of smart phones and portable computers).

- With the support of personalized and easier-to-use technological improvements (the Internet, the web, and call centers), customer started to talk directly to the members of supply chain in accordance to the service each of them provide.

---

wireless broadband access as an alternative to wired broadband like cable and digital subscriber line (DSL)."

[5] 3G is the third generation of mobile phone standards and technology, superseding 2.5G. It is based on the International Telecommunication Union (ITU, www.itu.int) family of standards under the IMT-2000.

[6] CDMA development group (www.cdg.org) explains: "Code Division Multiple Access (CDMA) is a spread spectrum technology, allowing many users to occupy the same time and frequency allocations in a given space. CDMA consistently provides better capacity for voice and data communications than other commercial mobile technologies, allowing more subscribers to connect at any given time, and it is the common platform on which 3G technologies are built."

According to the changes in the communication medium and their effectiveness, customers are more responsive and taking part in the evaluation of the service themselves. The Internet, its infrastructural integration to many personal devices, and its ability for interactivity break the old walls between organizations and customers and create new forms of dialogue.

There are some interesting examples of customer's advisory to mention: Many of the news and discussion TV-shows are delivering emails of their consumers directly to the computer in front of the moderator of the show, and let them participate, involve and evaluate the show presented. This method is the premier of this level customer involvement in the services. From this point on, it is easier to say that customers are more into the shaping of a service. Another example, as referred in its web site[7], is the strategy followed by Zara Inditex Fashion Company (Zara) when textile industry was having trouble in the

---

[7] Zara Inditex Fashion Company Web Site: www.zara.com, "the company" link

late 1990s. First, Zara got focused and made its business model around the customer. Second, Zara changed its slogan to "Offers dressing ideas, trends and tastes" to imply its closeness to customer expectations, its respect to individuality and its ability to be a part of the ideas and trends driven by customers. Third, Zara built an information system distributed in every store and working through the Internet by which sales force is connected directly to designers online to deliver market feedback about the fashion clothes. Zara still maintains this strategy as shown on their website: "... the customer is the centre of our particular business model, which integrates design, manufacture, distribution and sales through its network of shops. All processes, from creation of product, share the same objective: giving the customer the fashion they expect. Every day, Zara interprets, adapts and takes trends to millions of people..."

These examples are implying that reengineering the customer responses, involving them into the service design, letting them talk to the organization direct and listening them in detail, conquering the real wisdom that ignites innovation in service and use of this as knowledge are important for better achievement. However, these are not so easy to implement without an appropriate information system infrastructure that is based on the marketing technology tools and configured for the enhancement of organizational decision making. As a matter of fact, innovation is the key to enable new ways of thinking, producing and presenting of value to customers. The most affirmative solution to competition challenges comes from the idea of innovation. As, referred by Prof. Russell L. Ackoff in an interview article (Allio, 2003), Prof. Dr. Albert Einstein puts it, "Without changing our patterns of thought, we will not be able to solve the problems we created with our current patterns of thought", thinking-out-of-box and innovativeness are critical capabilities to remain competitive for any organization acting in the global markets.

Innovative corporate-thinking encompasses everything from derivation of meaningful customer insights to developing entirely new business models. For this reason, creation of an innovative mind-set starts at the strategic level decision-making. If innovative-thinking is appropriately captivated by people of the organization, it becomes a sustainable structure that delivers a better consumer experience and brings the rewards of loyalty and advisory. It supports the extension of loyal customer-base and capturing of new consumer markets. Apparently, it should therefore be a permanently dynamic internal process of organization in parallel with the delicately reception of changes in demand structures of the markets. Thus, makes innovative corporate-thinking to be considered in the elements of the model this research proposes.

2.3 Brand Communities as part of Customer's Advisory

The other component of the initial research model, brand community and its connection with service evaluation to strengthen the customer value and advisory role also requires attention. If customer's advisory is an important element of service evaluation, brand equity is one another because of the status it retains before the "lens" of the customer (Johnson and Gustafsson, 2000). In fact, brand community is the linkage between brand equity and customer's

39

advisory. Gobé (2002) mentions that issue with a good rephrase: "...It is about igniting the passion of customers so that they want to talk to the brand and to their friends about the brand. Once this passion is ignited, all the brand has to do is listen and act on what it learns from people! This model makes so much more sense because it means finding people who are really and truly interested in what the brand has to offer- it is a win-win situation" (p.199). For a better understanding, some more of the background of this particular subject is needed to be explored:

Brands are contemplated expositions of organizations. Unfortunately, brands are not merely belonging to organizations indeed, as Fisk (2006) underlined, brands are crafted by customers. They are sensitive to the impact on their customers' lives and make it their responsibility to enhance those lives in order to stay in there.

The awareness set of alternatives in the mind of consumer is expected to contain brands that consumer feel more accustomed to because of:

- semiotic subconscious information stored (Zaltman, 2003),

- believed in its satisfactory services as presented in integrated communication messages (Kitchen and Schultz, 2003)
- or had differentiated from others in the market by other means. (Porter, 1985)

These constraints push forward that getting the attention and staying there for longer require stimulation of internal information resources that consumer has a tendency to build a bonding relationship. For this purpose, by reversing the point of view to consumer insight, brands became matters of common interests shared by targeted audience who are willing to be customers. If brand is a medium of exposition of a comprehensive message from a service, then brand community is a group of customers that use, share interest, evaluate, recommend, advise and even admire, love, or advocate the brand. This community associates itself with brand and increases the brand equity as stressed by Aaker (1998).

Another importance of brand equity is the extension of brand anticipation to get appropriate positioning in consumer mind through presenting the associated values of brand and even virtues that it stands for (Ries and Trout, 1981). These are more important remarks that resemble in the mind of consumer that makes her a customer. The process of reaching to consumers with good timing and appropriate messages, painting a proper brand image in their minds and leaving a resemblance to stand until purchase decision, is getting harder without meaningful propositions of virtues or remarks of positive experience with brand.

Following the ideas of Silvie and Fetzer (2005) on community networks, other academicians focused on this concept for branding. Brand signification and its emphasis in community, conversation and cultural change have critical importance in the management of brand meaning, accumulated as "brand manifold" by Berthon et al (2007). The same concept is explained by Tek (2006) from a different perspective as "rituals" that have an important role for dissemination of information about how to experience that brand's value proposition better. Rituals, generally symbolic, are used by customers to create new perceptions, associate new meanings, relate old habits, or even build cultural connections with brand.

Muniz and O'Guinn (2001) defined brand community as non-geographically specialized social relations of admirers of brand. As a matter of fact, brand community, besides their definition, is dependent of brand manifold and rituals, connections, beliefs and traditions, and sharing information to and from brand. Moreover, it poses a continuum because brands have pasts, presents and futures in the mind of customer.

From this perspective, since customers could become recommenders or voluntary marketers of services, advisors or responsive service evaluators, and on the contrary, become dislikers or stoppers, an organization would need to understand its customers' needs and habits by employing effective marketing technology. This further helps to stop them turning into a disliker. Therefore, building the brand community for an elevation in brand equity is an additional contributing factor to the model. Brand community with its connection with service evaluation to strengthen the customer value and advisory role, strongly related with co-creation of value defined in service dominant logic of marketing approach (SDLM) by Lusch and Vargo (2004).

Customer's advisory presents an opportunity to scrutinize the contradiction of value-in-use and value-in-exchange (Proctor, 1991; Svoboda, 2006; Grönroos, 2008) discussed in the foundational premises of SDLM. For a comprehension, directions about the organization's limitations discussed for SDLM and issues debated by noteworthy scholars around the customer's co-creation of the value in the exchange are inductively related with evaluation of service. Moreover, with this point of view, the organization's single most ability is the proposition of value, not the value itself. Value of the service is defined by the customer, according to the ultimate utility that service resembles in its mind. By this way, customer acts so as it names the value of, consumes and disposes, advises and recommends the service. Even more, evaluation of service is also a service that customer executes in value co-creation of actual service.

2.4   Strategic Imperatives for Competition

Competitiveness of firms is highly based on the strategic imperatives. Firms pay great attention to attain customer satisfaction and loyalty while competing for better revenue margins and higher shareholder value. These two conflicting constraints are explained in the literature as superior customer value (Weinstein and Johnson, 1999) as first stated in the introduction (p.8) and superior financial performance (Hunt, 1997). Superior customer value refers to understanding and satisfying the needs of customers by solid interaction and collaboration, whereas superior financial performance is the outcome of corporate objectives with a focus on increasing market share, improving profitability, and attaining revenue growth. Both superiorities are the drivers to sustain competitive advantages for an organization.

As a result, superior customer value and superior financial performance are closely related and are amplified together if they are treated as constitutional blocks of innovative corporate-thinking for service evaluation. In Figure 1.1, the three dimensions of modern organization were stated. Further on this

45

issue, acquaintance of superior financial performance is a formulation of service development and organizational development where as superior customer value assessment is basically a function of service development and customer development as abbreviated below in Figure 2.1.

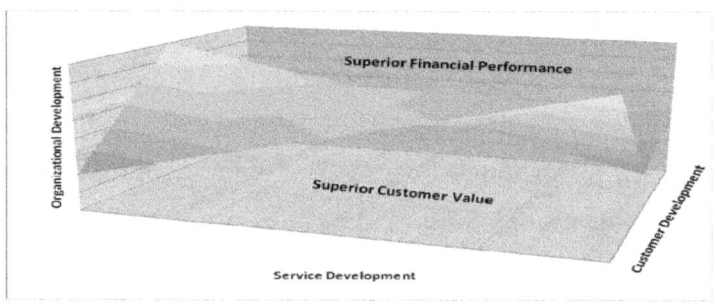

Figure 2.1 Three dimensions of modern organization including strategic imperatives

Customer's advisory is critical in competition for the next generation of customers those are more responsive to services market. As the product is getting more bundled with the service and responsibility of making difference in the market is more depending on the variety of services, quality and value are stressed more often. Gale (1994) defined a four stages model to make quality in services a strategic weapon for organizations. In his framework, total quality management and customer value management are integrated stepwise. He emphasized that market-perceived quality and value is relative to competitors in the market and therefore quality perceived by the customers is a key to customer value management.

On the other hand, according to Weinstein and Johnson (1999), superior customer value depends on perceived quality of service and also relative cost of it: There are various factors effecting on perceived quality imperative such as performance, attributes, aesthetics, reliability, durability, safety, better communication manners, easy and timely transaction, and post-purchase experience. As the organizations make value propositions, it is strategically important to associate such proposition with perceived quality and its relative cost.

Lusch and Vargo (2004) further compromise and extend the relationships of service and customer, as well as organizational knowledge development and quality management in the service dominant logic of marketing (SDLM) approach. As a matter of fact, for the effectiveness of customer's advisory interpretation

47

for organizations, there are several key factors from SDLM. The first one is, indicated by "goods are distribution mechanisms for service provision", related with how good goods are rendered by services. Those activities of the organization as to render the good with service are important to interact with customer. The second one is related with acceptance of the customer as a co-creator of value. Lusch and Vargo (2006a) emphasized in several of the debates throughout their book and placed as the sixth foundational premise of SDLM: "the customer is always co-creator of value" (p.4, p.18, p.44, and p.412). Their indication was that there are intervening factors between resources, resistances and collaboration. What they offer is a set of value co-creation activities, "to market with customers" rather than "to market to" (p.413), in: value proposition, service offering, processes for networking and dialogue in between organization and its customers.

With this premise in mind; if the customer defines the value at the time of consumption based on previous experience and perception, then involvement of customer becomes more critical to service evaluation.

According to Rosen (2000), innovative services create higher involvement than the ones that are not.

In addition, resource-advantage theory (Hunt, 1997) stresses that organizational learning and innovation is endogenous as the organizations and customers have imperfect information in the market. As organizational, informational and relational resources are heterogeneous and imperfectly mobile (Hunt, 1997), the organization is in need of customer's advisory for better relationship building with customer-base, learning from the experiences and retaining innovative ideas from at a lower cost. In connection with micro-specialization (Lusch and Vargo, 2004) and advantages of better resources, the organization develops the capability of better performance (Hunt and Morgan, 1997).

The competition is bringing forward the problems related with differentiation, focusing, finding niches and out-of-box thinking. Customer-oriented strategies address the importance of perceived quality that conquers product, associated service and experience, the importance of customer lifetime value that inhabits co-creation of value "to market with customers" and the importance of brand communities which is a contemporary form of controlling the word-of-mouth. Strategic imperatives of superior customer value and superior financial performance are assessed through use of marketing technology tools and reception of customer's advisory for evaluation of services with innovative corporate thinking.

2.5 Marketing Technology and Synthesis of Strategic Imperatives

The rapid movement of the market conditions with globalization challenges, increasing number of actors entering competition and dynamism in consumer behavior generate a vortex of uncertainty in markets (Fisk, 2006). Thus, the responses of decision-makers and consumers trigger more reciprocal responses in a complex web with halo effect. While consumers are affected by many messages, and are exposed to many sources, they also have effects on others more than before with the support of more advanced communication tools. These tools are technology based and provide an extended way of understanding the market than before.

The challenge for organizations is a result of technological advancements which empower ordinary consumer to become intelligent and questioning, responsive and lauder in the classical word-of-mouth communication. Ridderstrale and Nordström (2000) mentioned: "The Web enables total transparency. People with access to relevant information are beginning to challenge any type of authority. The stupid, loyal and humble customer, employee, patient or citizen is dead" (p.102). It is clear that, Internet brings out an opportunity for organizations having detailed conversations with customers, listening to their comments about services offered, collection of their feedbacks about fulfillment of the service, and even how to improve the service to reach a superior customer value.

Lusch and Vargo (2004) also underline how knowledge is essential for organizations as a component of differentiation and source of competitive advantage. According to Tiwana (2001), "knowledge management lets you challenge what you know, and redesign and reconfigure existing products and services to radically

51

transform their value proposition to meet new customer needs" (p.43). From this point of view, knowledge management opens a new gateway from what is collected as data to transformation of service for customer. Even more, it facilitates a change in the service for the untapped market. Therefore, integration of knowledge management practices into relationship management processes brings out the possibilities of success in closer customer interaction, customized product design and configured service.

As a matter of fact, marketing runs on technology. Nevertheless, most marketing and technology organizations are separately evolved and not very well aligned to work together effectively. These two organizations plan and budget differently, measure success differently, and have widely different cultures. Many customer-driven organizations need new ways to align marketing and information technologies to develop better targeted marketing campaigns, integrated efficient systems and detailed customer analytics. In their findings, Thomas et al. (2004) identify that relative impact of retention versus acquisition investments on customer is a complicated question of finding the right balance. They indicate that reaching the optimal balance is more important than finding the optimum amount to invest for profitable customer groups.

It is not only gathering reliable information about the internal processes of the organization for better measurement, but also using it to "out-think" rivals is important. Analytics, which is the acronym for sophisticated quantitative and statistical analysis and predictive modeling, is one of the most powerful tools to make managerial decisions. The Internet and its impact on the change of every day devices in ordinary customer's life, brings out many opportunities to collect data impossible to deliver a few years ago. According to Gobé (2002) and Payne and Frow (2005), this will only continue to grow as the process becomes even more streamlined and refined. Therefore, organizations are faced to build their competitive strategies around data-driven insights that in turn generate impressive results. Some examples of using analytics have been mentioned by Davenport and Harris (2007): identification of the most profitable customers and offering them right price, acceleration of product and service innovation, optimization of supply chains, and identification of the true drivers of financial performance. Payne and Frow (2005) have also mentioned the anticipation of profitable customers for determination of right price as a result of an analysis about the likelihood of the customer to respond an offer by the organization. Several studies (Aydın et. al, 2000; Güngör and Aktoluğ, 2007) have also focused on the supply chain optimization, financial drivers of performance in customer-driven supply chains and calibration of attributes and messages for offerings to elicit synchronization in unified demand planning process of cascaded supply chains.

Turning information collected from customers to organizational wisdom is not an easy task. It is dependent on various factors from the operational view such as an organizational culture that listens to customers critically, covering the right compound of rational and emotional needs of customer, observation and logging, and understanding ethnographic reasons (Whitney, 1989).

Many of the organizations collect data in discrete systems. Some of them combine those sources of data and build data warehouses. And some of those even build data mining and in-depth analysis tools for their business intelligence (Frey, 2001). All of these are technically acceptable but true contribution of these analyses comes from the right questions to be asked by marketing or management teams to such systems. Moreover, these systems are mostly based on statistics, only some of them provide stochastic analyses. Holistic and expert system approaches are fairly new (Aramburu and Saenz, 2007).

Even more organizations are in need of collecting responses from customers in various forms, storing them in classified groups of data before drilling into it. A query about the mean of customer age is simple and easy to retrieve. But, there is much to do with this data such as reading its context to set up a semantic search into it to determine what the customer really meant about the service in between the lines of its writing or voice recording.

In such circumstances, organizations are in need of demystification of both open and hidden commentary in customer responses to make them decision-making arguments. Implementation of marketing technology tools for complex decision-cubes requires good modeling of organizational needs, good assembly of customer touch points and good modeling for knowledge management of comprehensive data warehouses and intelligent business tools to synthesize the strategic imperatives from customer's advisory for innovative service evaluation.

From inside the core to the outside brand communities, the organization incorporates critical technological components that make a comprehensive marketing decision support system (Wierenga et al., 1999; Van Bruggen et al., 2001): data warehousing, database marketing tools, enterprise resource planning tools, human resource management systems, supply chain management tools, customer relationship management tools, business intelligence systems and call center management systems. Supporting easier collection of internal and external data and enabling visual presentation in different user environments, web based solutions are in the mainstream: intranets, extranets, internet web sites, blogs, and emailing tools. Although each specialized marketing technology tool could act standalone, they are capable of being integrated seamlessly to act as a decision support system. Therefore, the implementations of these tools are independent from the size of the organization as they are scalable in accordant to the need.

In sum, it can be stated that in customer-oriented approach, the basic premise is providing better customer value and it is hardly mistakable to remain competitive. SDLM emphasize that co-creation of value with customer helps both to increase customer satisfaction, higher involvement of brand communities. The use of marketing technology for "customer development" and the analysis of customer's advisory provide the capability to adaptive organizations for efficient communication processes that bring out valuable results to improve their services.

3 CONCEPTUAL MODEL

Contribution of customers to organizational value development is in form of customer involvement and customer's advisory. Cram (2001) describes customer involvement as the act of customers as a form of personal advertisement, voluntary unofficial sales-force, and referrer on organization's behalf.

This definition explains the direction of involvement: Customer is not generally considered as a part of the organization and as an outsider. Customer involves in brand, product or service of the organization and disseminates information about these to other customers. From Cram's perspective, such customers are also assets and to capitalize on these assets, a systematic information flow must be assured. Customer involvement is an important marketing tool for the organization to keep up, but on the other hand customer's advisory is another one that takes a step further for the evaluation of services and brings in reverse direction of involvement into brand, product or service.

There is a critical difference of customer's advisory from customer involvement: customer's advisory has the power to trigger dynamics of the organization from inside out. Its impact in the evaluation of service is more direct to pass in all dimensions of modern organization simultaneously.

Gobé (2002) characterizes this as "active consumerism" to define the attitude of customers who personally involve in the equity of brand by positive responses. This, as he underlines, is a result of encouragement for active engagement of customers. Customer's advisory is related with "active consumerism" as it is an enhancement of customer involvement put to action.

In this book, the core concept stands for the understanding of organizational capabilities for using marketing technology tools to formulate their strategic imperatives (superior customer value and superior financial performance) through customer's advisory. Making use of customer's advisory necessitates focusing on two main elements: being open to listen to customers (Openness), and being capable of service evaluation (Capability). The use of "customer's advisory" in an organization depends on the existence of these two components.

3.1 "Openness": being open to customers, listening to their advisory and analyzing their responses

Organizations are required to be listening to the customer if they are supposed to collect valuable responses and derive insights from customer's advisory. A comprehension of such openness is related with three major organizational behaviors:

organization is willing to listen to the markets, organizational culture is appropriate, and technology is enabled for customer's advisory reception. Berry and Parasuraman (1997, p.65) address the issue as "To improve service, companies must use multiple research approaches among different customer groups to ensure that they are hearing what customers are saying and responding to their suggestions."

Parasuraman and Grewal (2000b) also indicate that there is a need for effective management of organization, employee and customer relationships together with technology. In correspondence to the pyramid model Parasuraman proposed in 1995, they extend the discussion with the analysis of linkages between technology and customer, technology and employee, and technology and company. Based on this approach, listening to the customer is related with three constructs to be taken into consideration: responsiveness, empathy and technology focus. The first two are related with the service quality measure to close the gap of communication between customers and the organization, and the third one is related with systematic capturing and analysis customer responses.

a. Responsiveness: willingness to help customers
b. Empathy: Individualized attention the organization provides to customer

Zeithaml et al. (1996) address five dimensions of service quality measurement, SERVQUAL, as: tangibles, reliability, responsiveness, assurance, and empathy. SERVQUAL aims to measure the gap between customer expectations and experience through a sequential series of smaller gaps proposed in Parasuraman et al (1991a). As these authors pointed out, from those gaps, the fourth one is related with effectiveness of communication with customer. Responsiveness and empathy are considered from this perspective and the measures developed by Parasuraman et al. (1991a) are adopted in this book. The definition of responsiveness put forward as "the willingness to help customers and provide prompt service", and empathy is explained as the care and individualized attention provided by an organization to its customers. It is apparent that for any organization to be open to its customers, responsiveness and empathy are the essential components.

c. Technology focus[8] to capture and analyze customer responses

Following the insights from the definition by Bartels (1965), decision support systems for marketing managers was stressed by Little (1979). As organizations develop the ability to learn and transform that learning into action rapidly, technology focus becomes the best competitive advantage. Serving for this aim, the number of different marketing decision support system tools incorporated in an organization affects collection, analysis and in turn listening to

---

[8] Parasuraman (2000a) defines technology readiness index (TRI) for the consumer side. According to TRI, a scale for measurement of customer reactions to technology described and constructed. In this study, "technology focus" indicates the readiness of the organizations to gather and make use of information through appropriate marketing technology tools as being open to customers, and "technology capability" indicates the capacity and the ability of the organizations to facilititate information gathered, to make use of information.

63

valuable customer responses. There are two major distinctions: first, internally configured to collect, store and execute as marketing decision support system tool (depicted as technology capacity of the organization for service evaluation); second, externally configured to present information and collect direct responses from customers online as e-business tool. The list of marketing technology tools states the details about the technological focus of the organization to capture and analyze customer responses were grouped as E-Business, below:

- E-Business (for Direct Communication with Customer) Tools

Nambisan and Nambisan (2008) discuss "virtual customer environment initiatives" that offer benefits beyond the innovation outcomes and shape customer and organization relationships under product related issues and the brand itself. They determine this requirement as follows: "the benefits of engaging customers in product development, product support and related activities are increasingly visible. Having the right technology-based system can enhance the customer experience and help companies improve both their innovation and customer relationship management capabilities" (p.53).

Following this issue, the right technology-based system consists of elements belonging both MDMSS and latent E-Business interaction facilitation tools to be incorporated for this purpose:

i. Web sites

Web sites are generally designed to express the vision and the functions of the organization to the public. Together with these, web sites are used for marketing and sales operations, interactive relationship with customers and partners, sharing information about organizational development, public relations, and social networking (Marsden, 2008). Web sites contain most of the functionalities of organization in physical world. Moreover, they carry out the extensions (such as entertainment, file sharing, digital communities, worldwide mobility of data distribution) brought by the features of virtual world.

ii. Direct communication tools

E-Business is the representation of business activities of any organization on the virtual worlds of communication. The most common platform for e-business is the Internet but mobile platforms and digital broadcasting platforms are also new mediums for e-business activities. The functions provided over these various platforms are generally have the same content with different interfaces:

• Interaction with brand communities

• E-Mailing

Organizations use complex e-mailing tools to comprehend text based messaging with customers, partners, and other parties. Organizations provide information to outer parties and customers through inexpensive e-mailing tool. One of the most common uses of e-mailing is low-density dialogue-based information exchange among people. Another important use of e-mailing is push and pull marketing communication. The drawback of e-mailing is many uninteresting e-mail content that is pushed to people without permission which decreases effectiveness of each new e-mail message (Merisavo and Raulas, 2004).

- Chat messaging

A better form of dialogue on the Internet is free of charge chatting in different forms: text-based, voice based or visual based. Organizations use these marketing technology tools for interactive messaging with customers and partners (Mayzlin, 2006; Van Dolen et al., 2007)

- Customer Forums

Electronic forums are used for sharing information over a discussion topic with a group of customers or partners (Gopal et al, 2006). There are two types of electronic forums (Bickart and Schindler, 2001): controlled and uncontrolled. The former one is maintained by the organization itself. The benefits of controlled forum are (Dellarocas, 2006): an easy way to collect views about services and it serves for building focus groups in low-cost and in many different locations at the same time.

Uncontrolled forums exist on the Internet and the organization could not act to set rules for the content (Harrison-Walker, 2001). The benefits of uncontrolled forum would be monitoring the discussions of consumer community about the brand

and capturing the clues for the evaluation of services.

- Blogging out the organization's services and support of brand manifold

Blogging is one of the newest ways people and organizations are using to express themselves out to an audience all over the world (Dwyer, 2007). Organizations use blogging to build intimacy with consumer community generally in the form of presenting their employees' daily talks about services or CEO's confessions and unconditional projections (Luo, 2007; Thelwall, 2008).

3.2 "Capability" of service evaluation

Prior researches (Menon and Varadarajan, 1992; Maltz and Kohli, 1996) indicate that product and service knowledge utilization and evaluation within organization were depending on characteristics of organization such as having computerized information systems, increased personal contacts, innovation orientation, market intelligence dissemination effectiveness, inter-personal trust, and communication between marketing and other business units. As a compromise, Fisher et al. (1997) found two significant measurement constructs in their study for evaluation capacity of organizations that indicate communication effectiveness in marketing and production units, which bring in an understanding opportunity for organizational readiness to the changes in market conditions. These two constructs were also tested by Massey and Kyriazis (2007) with an integrative structural model:

a. Bidirectional information-sharing in marketing and production / engineering units
b. Frequency in information use by production / engineering units for service evaluation

Furthermore, facilitation of information sharing between organizational units depends on installment of appropriate marketing technology tools to set proper capacity of information flow and storage. For this reason, a third construct called "technology capacity" was considered in the research model.

c. Technology capacity of the organization to evaluate services and innovation

Internal tools for setting up organizational capacity for service evaluation were grouped as Marketing Decision Making Support Systems (MDMSS), and listed below.

- Marketing Decision Making Support Systems (MDMSS)

   Van Bruggen et al. (2001) conclude, while explaining the marketing and technology relationship that, over the years sophisticated tools were developed in both information technology and marketing science and started to be used by marketers. They were called marketing management support systems

(MMSS), a combination of information technology, analytical capabilities, marketing related data and marketing knowledge interpretation. These systems started as marketing information systems in 1960s (Van Bruggen et al., 2001) and extended to marketing knowledge-based systems and marketing neural nets of 1990s.

On the other hand, as defined by AMA web site, a decision support system from marketing research point of view is "A coordinated collection of data, system tools, and techniques with supporting software and hardware by which an organization gathers and interprets relevant information from business and the environment and turns it into a basis for making management decisions".

Based on the discussion of Van Bruggen et al. (2001) and AMA (2008), a marketing decision making support system (MDMSS) is a combination of complex sub-systems of each collect different aspects of operational data, track organizational progress, store customer transactions and relations, retain external environmental responses of markets and seamlessly integrate such discrete information when needed for a marketing decision-making process in various managerial levels. Wierenga et al. (1999) note this understanding as "...tendency towards companywide information systems with integrated modules for different functional areas such as production, logistics, marketing, and finance (so called ERP systems)" (p.205). They call this system the interdependence of marketing and research and development, stress that it is fostering the relationship between marketing strategy and technology strategy.

As a matter of fact, MDMSS is composed of complex sub-systems. These sub-systems related to activation of customer's advisory in form of reception, storage, analysis and evaluation of information from customers relate to the following areas (Wierenga et al, 1999; Van Bruggen et al., 2001; Tiwana, 2001; Holsapple, 2005; Afiouni, 2007): customer relationship management, enterprise resource planning and human resource management systems.

i. Customer Relationship Management (CRM)

CRM is a management methodology which places the customer at the center of organizational activities. It is based on the use of technologies for collection, process and analysis of information related to the customers. Stuart (2005) defines CRM as "Creating customer relationships through a consistent, relevant dialogue across multiple channels in order to maximize customer satisfaction and business results" (p.42). There are two major fractions in CRM tools: operational and analytical. Operational CRM deals with the integration of the front office organizational processes that are in contact with customer where as analytical CRM uses data mining techniques over the information related with the customers of the organization. A latest approach of collaborative CRM is emerging through the integration with business processes with customer relations where

74

operational and analytical CRM functionalities are used extensively. Typical CRM software includes customer data management, contact and campaign management, proposal and order management, sales force automation, and marketing resource management features. In many of CRM technologies today, database marketing is embedded as functionality for targeted marketing activities. According to Stuart (2005), the most popular CRM components in the order of the level of commitment are data analytics for customer research, marketing and sales automation, channel integration, email response management, sales force automation and website personalization from the user's point of view.

ii. Enterprise Resource Planning (ERP)

ERP consists of one or a set of software applications that integrate information and processes across the several organizational functions. Typically, ERP integrates planning, procurement, sales, marketing, customer relationship, finance and human resources. Van Bruggen et al. (2001) claim that organization wide information systems such as ERP enhance inter-departmental information sharing. By this way, marketers get access to data from production and vice versa. This knowledge transmission increases the availability of data for the support of marketing decision making and marketing insights.

iii. Human Resource Management System for Performance Measurement (HRMS)

HRMS is the strategic and coherent approach to the management of an organization's people who individually and collectively contribute to the achievement of the objectives of the organization. Roos et. al. (2004) underline the relationships between strategic intent, cultural behavior and business processes in an organization, performance measurement is placed in the intersection of all three. Afiouni (2007) extends this approach with its linkages to resource-based view of the firm and knowledge management efficiency. Human resource performance measurement is the process of calculating the level of personal targets and the level of achievements in order to find how successful those personnel are for a specific period. It is closely related with organizational performance (Roos et al., 2004), and financial performance (Pietsch, 2007). Pietsch (2007) discussed that the ambiguity in measurement of human capital shall be avoided by not promoting "opportunistic patterns of behavior in offering opportunities" (p.265) to the people and so that institutionalization and effective framing could be employed to standardize measures and to avoid uncertainty in added value calculation of human resources. Schiemann (2006) calls this valuation concept as "people equity" of the organization and notes that management and measurement of this equity as an investment is critical importance to the organization. From this perspective, the importance of HRMS which allow organizations to automate many aspects of human resource management with additional benefits of reducing workload of related departments as well as increasing the efficiency by standardization of processes, is obvious (Roos et. al, 2004; Afiouni, 2007; Pietsch, 2007).

Taking the arguments of Holsapple (2005) and Afiouni (2007) into consideration, HRMS convert human resources information into digitally traceable format to be added to the knowledge management systems of organization. As Bygdås et al. (2004) pointed out, "Performance measurement and management in firms where knowledge is the central strategic resource provide composite challenges. Not only are the knowledge resources tacit, collective, complex, deeply rooted in culture and hard to imitate and transfer, but the processes of value creation and their outputs are also of a more or less intangible nature". By this way, HRMS plays an important role in ensuring easy running of an organization by tracking and analyzing the performance and work patterns of the workforce, supporting management with better information to form strategies.

iv.   Intranet System that supports sharing and discussion of customer's advisory within the organizational units and supports feedbacks of internal customers. An Intranet system is a web based technology to be accessed by the stakeholders of the organization internally for sharing information in secure and closed-loop environment.

So, making use of customer's advisory is related to interactions of customer with organization, organizational responsiveness and empathy by being open to customers, being technologically ready to capture customer responses, feedback and advisory prompt, being able to make it recorded correctly, and an organizational operation capability to evaluate the service.

3.3 Construction of "Openness" and "Capability"

From customer point of view, the product is a mean of satisfaction to a need or motivation and the service is the overall presentation of the product (Lusch and Vargo, 2006). The successful evaluation in service or innovation is associated with organizational experience and learning (Sawhney et al., 2006), service observation, the study of competing services, regulative obligations, as well as careful research on the service considering customer perspectives. In fact, one of the best sources of information for evaluation of the service is the well communicated customer, i.e. the user of that service.

From the organization's point of view, it is becoming critical to develop understanding different organizational units where the use of certain technological tools can also help for the communication with customers, by the increasing support of technology and customer's adaptation to use this technological support better. Thus, brings us an opportunity of observing classical theories of word-of-mouth (Katz and Lazarsfeld, 1955) and halo effect, in action.

3.3.1 Customer insight utilization

The requirement of customer-oriented strategies for organizations imposes the capabilities to extend the horizons of three dimensions in Figure 1.1. Organizations generally limit themselves with internal insights from employees and managers or past experiences while making extensions to these dimensions. However, one of the most important resources of innovation is generally untapped or under stressed: customers. Customers have experiences with the service and save them in their memories, form engrams and distribute information about the service. They develop insights about the service. Clauser (2001, p.276) phrases this subject from strategic point of view, "... customer insight is the foundation for growing and developing consumers in the e-world and underpins brand strategy".

i. Customer lifetime value and customer retention (Reichheld, 1996; Day, 1999; Tek, 2006)

- Time length spend with the brand
- Frequency of purchase of the brand

Reichheld (1996) found these critical from the customer satisfaction angle. Later on, Day (1999) underlined this issue in detail from the market dynamics point of view. Finally, explanations of Tek (2006) about the importance of customer value and CLV for the modern organization are also very comprehensive.

ii. Co-creation of value (Lusch and Vargo, 2004)

- Value-in-Use or Value-in-Exchange (Lusch and Vargo, 2004)
- Brand communities (Muniz and O'Guinn, 2001)

One of the foundational premises of SDLM fosters the idea about the determination of value. Lusch and Vargo (2004), point out that it

82

is always a function performed by the customer and so it is called value-in-use, rather than value-in-exchange that is embedded by the manufacturing. Supporting this idea, Grönroos (2004) explains in his discussion about customer-organization touch points, that value proposition of organization is bounded to the customer value process. With this in mind, if the value is defined by the customer, then the customer surely would like to involve in the service and possibly contribute its evaluation.

Moreover, from the explanations of Aaker (1998) about building the brand equity to the discussions of Muniz and O'Guinn (2001) about how brand communities involve in elevation of this equity, following the ancient word-of-mouth theories of Katz and Lazarsfeld (1955), value-in-use is defined and shared with brand community more often and easier by the help of 21st century's E-business tools.

iii. One-to-one relations with customers (Grönroos, 2004)

The relation to customers can be build through two basic units in the organization where personal and one-to-one dialogue and interaction with customers are essential tasks for:

- Sales force (Speier and Venkatesh, 2002)
- Call Center agents (Beaujean et al., 2006)

As the customer calls in or visits the store, it is welcomed by sales force in general or call center agent. Grönroos (2004) indicates a framework of central processes in relationship marketing which holds interaction process as the core and a planned communication process as the distinct media towards customer's value processes to merge a relationship. Beaujean et al. (2006) emphasize that "the spark between customer and frontline staff members helps transformation of skeptical people into strong and committed brand followers". Therefore, it is presented as in the hypothesis below, the human interaction with customers is considered in merging a relationship to enable customer's advisory.

3.3.2 Human resources advantages relative to market

In Hunt's proceedings, resource-advantage theory of competition is presented, challenged, debated and explained: "social structures can be competition enhancing" (Hunt and Arnett, 2003) where specifically human resources are considered.

i. Quality in talent of organization by education relative to the human resource market

ii. Quality in talent of organization by experience relative to the human resource market

If any organization is better equipped with human resources to listen to the customer, then this would be an advantage in the competition as well. As long as the organization gets better with learning by education and from experience (Hoch and Deighton, 1989), it attains the capability to understand its customer's advisory as well. Knowledge level and experience level of human resources in an organization are also important factors in innovativeness regardless of the cultural and managerial differences between countries (Uysal, 2009).

3.3.3 Knowledge resource interpretation capability

Hunt and Arnett (2003) also addressed informational resources as knowledge from consumer and competitive intelligence to support the constitution of competitive advantage in the marketplace. Carlucci and Schiuma (2006) underlined that organization's value proposition was bounded with its knowledge resource interpretation capability to identify casual dynamics of interdependencies in organization's environment.

The utilization of firm's knowledge resources to backfire incompleteness in organizational tasks and procedures are important. On the other hand, this indicates that the wisdom reconstructed from customer's advisory in the form of informational resource within the marketing decision support systems is subject to superior financial performance. Therefore, development of knowledge resources and converting these resources into "dynamic capability of market responsiveness" (Griffith et al. ,2006) is crucial for the organization to remain competitive.

3.3.4 Innovative corporate-thinking

In their recent paper Bettencourt and Ulwick (2008)
introduce the customer-centered innovation map with
a systematic and process based point of view. They
specify sub-processes a consumer executes in
consummating any service and highlight possibilities
of innovation in each sub-process to make consumer
more satisfied. This approach opens up many chances
of improvement in the services that an organization
proposes value to its customers if it has an innovative-
corporate thinking mindset. In-depth understanding of
"customer's advisory" is more than ignition of
innovation or detection of service evaluation
possibilities; it fosters exploration of new attributes
and challenging the functionalities of existing services
and therefore incorporates the innovative-corporate
thinking for making these services better fit for the
customer. This customization expands:

i.   in design of service

ii. in management

iii. in customer relations

Investigation about better functionalities in the services of competitors, research of new attributes for enhancement of services and exploration of new ideas are all related with innovative corporate-thinking. Grönroos (2004) underlines that relationships are important for an organization, but relationship building is not an easy task to realize successfully. As the customer behavior changes by the time or by the effects in socio-economic environment, the organization would be receptive to these changes to stay in the game of competition. Such parallel changes require innovative culture in management and design of service within organization.

The use of marketing technology for listening to customer's advisory is aimed to make use of it for the direction to achieve superior financial performance and superior customer value. These two strategic imperatives are the ultimate goals of any organization to realize in competitive global environment. As consequences, these imperatives are related with growth and long-term success of the organization.

On one hand, the use of marketing technology for relieving customer's advisory into a new feature addition to products and innovation in service design, specifically related to empowerment of customer and customer related organizational culture. As the internal drivers of the organization are captive and proactive to customer's responses, the innovative culture is able to be established in the organization. This change of the core - from processes to customer – is a major strategic movement.

On the other hand, human resources, knowledge gained from the information flow from internal and external stakeholders, building advanced relationships, increasing the effectiveness in communication are all encountered through proper implementation of required marketing technology tools. The number of these tools is increasing as the technology advances. Digitalization of many existing products like TV broadcasting, cars and white goods support the new data generation touch points where customer can instantly inform the service provider just by the use of the service. Mobility of customer brings in new opportunities of using information sources about the location and offered service where better relationship marketing strategies can be redirected promptly. All channels are gaining the capability of hearing the customer voice, understanding between the lines of customer's responses and interpretation of innovative ideas in customer's feelings and thoughts about the brand, and customer's advisory about services offered by the organization.

The organization's ownership type (private or publicly listed), hierarchy structure (flat or steep) and size (in Top 500, number of employees, or total revenue) are some of its critical internal factors defining overall context of the organization. Moreover, some explanatory variables were used to make analysis and explain dichotomous effects of this specific phenomenon, customer's advisory, based on differences in clusters of data. These variables were: perceived competitiveness by the managers in the main sector of organization and business orientation of organization (B2C or B2B)

In summary, the organizations aim to reach two major goals together with some others. These two are, superior financial performance (Hunt, 1997) and superior customer value (Weinstein and Johnson, 1999), considered as starting points of initial research model, from a top-down design. This research aims to determine acting factors of the use of marketing technology to capture and make use of customer's advisory and seeks for the explanation of independent, moderating and explanatory variables upon such factors, the initial model represents this affection and their reliance.

A success factor for a modern organization is the efficient use of marketing technology to capture and make use of customer advisory, among other success factors. In this book, the upcoming importance of the customer relationship with the organization is stressed in the introduction. The reasons behind the drivers of this relationship are not only limited to strategic basis in competition but also extended to the value proposition and exchange fundamental of marketing science redefined by the works of Lusch and Vargo (2004). Customer's advisory, which has the potential to trigger innovation in the most convenient and low-cost manner, is gaining critical importance.

According to previous works of many scholars pointed in the literature survey, the dependent variable formation is composed of two main parts: openness to listen to customer's advisory, responses and feedback; capability to service evaluation. If any organization is able to get precisely the impulses of information from the consummators of its services, that would be the first aspect of the dependent variable. Besides, the organization is required to have the capability to evaluate its services to make better use of this wisdom coming directly from fine users of its services. The dependent variable is a component of these two major aspects where each has sub-dimensions.

Openness to listen to customer responses is a matter of responsiveness, empathy and technological focus. Organizations are sending tremendous amount of messages to their audience, and they are also receiving many messages from their customers. Their responsiveness and empathy (defined by Parasuraman et. al 1991b in SERVQUAL constructs) are critical to anticipate problems, change requests, ideas, recommendations of their customer as well as understanding some of the changes in the consumer market. In addition, technological focus and technological capacity are also requirements for organizations to get these relationship transactions with customers and make a proper use of them for strategic benefit of organization. E-Business components such as web sites and other direct communication tools like E-mails, Blogs, and Forums were tools incorporated by organizations to establish better communication with customer community.

Over the capability of service evaluation in organizations there exist several crucial requirements to calculate if they are effective in making use of customer's advisory: bidirectional information-sharing and the frequency in information use among the engineering and marketing departments in the organization to be incorporated for evaluation of services. Marketing technology tools called "marketing decision making support systems" that include CRM Technologies, ERP System, HRMS and Intranet system.

The use of customer insight utilization, human resource advantages, knowledge interpretation and innovative corporate-thinking are composite independent variables effective on the dependent. Customer insight utilization includes customer lifetime and retention, co-creation of value, and one-to-one relations with customers through sales force and call center agents. Human resources advantages of organization are measured by quality in talent pool of the organization relative to competitors in the market. This quality is dependent to the average level of education and average experience level of the personnel employed by the organization. Knowledge resource interpretation and evaluation capability addresses the ability of organization to use knowledge as a tool for competition to understand and face with the dynamics of markets. Finally, innovative corporate-thinking is composed of three distinct paths to focus organizational innovativeness: design, management and relations.

Nevertheless, while dependent variable is under the effect of changes in independent variables, there are moderating and explanatory variables to be considered. Moderation over this affection is related with classification of organization through its type, structure and size. Explanatory variables were related with the sector of the organization, competition sought by the managers of the organization and core business orientation of the organization.

4 DISCUSSIONS

4.1 Organizational Adaptiveness to Useful Impulses from Customer

There are three major issues related with "Organizational Adaptiveness to Useful Impulses from Customer" to understand the importance of customer value and extension of it:

1. customer value creation
2. linking customer value with consumer network
3. extending customer value over the organizational value-chain.

As discussed in Smith and Colgate (2007), the idea of a framework for customer value creation rooted from customer value paradigm, also stated by Hunt and Morgan (1997) as, "the objective of marketing is to achieve personal, organizational and societal objectives by creating superior customer value" (p.7). Smith and Colgate (2007) insist on that customer value research is "still in early stages of conceptual development" (p.7). From this perspective, as creation of value for customers is a critical task when evaluating services or developing new ones, Smith and Colgate (2007) define a conceptual framework to design new marketing strategies, recognizing new opportunities, and enhancing existing service concept specifications. Definition of customer value framework was stated as a generalization by the evaluation of each component such as types of value, sources, environment, interactions and products for every organization in different forms. Value creation is a customized process for any organization and should be directed under a scope drawn by the long term strategies of the organization itself. According to Lusch and Vargo (2004), co-creation of value is a dominant determinator in modern marketing strategies for services. For this reason, an organization is responsible of sustainability in creating value propositions together with their customers and following a proper systematic accustomed for itself.

Following value creation, linking its proposition result with consumer network is also important. Regarding this issue, Bowman and Narayandas (2004) pointed out the critic of how to adapt and extend value in network as the development of useful guidelines for customer management efforts in the organization.

Tseng et al. (2007) posed the requirement of delivering superior value to customers in competitive markets is wrapped around the strategies using consumer networks efficiently. They noted two elements in the context of network effects: increasing total customer value and reducing total customer costs. Increase in total customer value is a function of increasing network size such as attracting more customers, horizontal integration of networks, strategic alliances, and increasing unit network value as "designing more valuable new services by enhancing communication with consumers" (p.46).

Another comment on this issue is also related with SDLM, suggested by Cova and Salle (2008), over the

97

application of the SDLM conceptual framework to co-create value in consumer networks based on a switch from customer value proposition to customer network value proposition. Cova and Salle (2008) put the solutions provided as services by organization in the center of customer network, supply network and co-creation of value process (p.271).

Finally, Mascarenhas et al. (2004) contributed the third stage of "Organizational Adaptiveness to Useful Impulses from Customer" as extending customer value over the organizational value-chain. Mascarenhas et al. (2004) indicated that traditional marketing strategies assumed customer involvement with services placed at the very end of the value-chain as "finished marketing offerings" (p.487). However, the role of customer is changing in the direction of more centralized manner in the involvement process. By this way, customer value and value chain gets more integrated over the involvement and contribution of customer with customer's advisory to the organizational processes of service evaluation. Mascarenhas et al. (2004) underlined this progress as "It can provide continuous customer feedback and enable more objective quality assessment and judgment, but most importantly, it can elevate customer satisfaction to customer delight that spawns lifetime loyalty and positive referrals" (p.489).

4.2 Marketing Technology Tools Ease Access to Customers and Emphasize Their Advisory Role

From the definitions of Bartels (1965), marketing technology was a technique and thought of marketing knowledge; "The concept of marketing knowledge as a technology has useful implications. Marketing practice developed as a technique; marketing thought developed as a technology" (p.46). From 1965 to 2008, there have been a lot of changes, improvements and developments in marketing science. The basis of marketing technology evolved in the appreciation of more technology into marketing thought and the use of so many technologies together with marketing thought. However, the foundations were defined as "for purposes of action in business situations-

99

particularly for the making of administrative decisions" (Bartels, 1965, p.45) still stands tall in 21st century.

One of the results claimed that the use of web sites for the interactivity of communication between organizations and customers is affirmative. Thus, brings in the emphasis of Bartels in 1965 as "relationships among components of the marketing channel" (p.47) for the flow of transactional information and "marketing technology is integrated with other technologies in achievement of overall corporate objectives" (p.47) for better managerial decision-making were inherited into 2008. In this extension, interactivity of direct communication web sites and social networking of the organization should take several important aspects into account to stay comprehensive, as explained by Center for Marketing Technology in Bentley University[9]: online shopping, online privacy, online customer satisfaction, auctions, personalization in wireless world, social rituals, information technology and marketing productivity,

---

[9] http://www.bentley.edu/cmt/research.cfm

100

marketing ethics in the information age, and relationship marketing strategies.

Ozuem et al. (2008) and Kalaignanam et al. (2008) indicated that computer mediated marketing environments and Internet frameworks provide organizations with a medium that can be used to deliver content in variety of ways to consumers and increase marketing operation efficiency. Thus, interpreted as the opportunity of integrating customized and different online web site interfaces, supports personalized marketing communication tactics to reach every individual. Additionally, Simmons (2008) underlines that there are complexities in postmodern consumer markets where consumers are individualistic and reliant to brand communities. Simmons (2008) identifies that "the Internet as an enabling tool which allows direct, real-time individualized interaction with postmodern consumers" (p.301).

Interactive web sites, opt-in responsive e-mailing, social network blogging, e-chatting and extranet sites of organizations lead the way to increase efficiency and effectiveness of organizational marketing resources by alignment of human resources and technology that decrease the time spent on planning, production and measurement of marketing communication activities. By this way, customers are enabled to use marketing technology tools easily and could emphasize their advisory role better.

4.3 Brand Communities Enhance Customer's Advisory and Customer Value

Based on the ideas of Cova and Salle (2008), there are two steps in processing the brand community's value proposition those have to be taken into consideration: identification of contributors in the consumer network and setting up a value co-creation approach with each customer. The result of implementation of a strategy in the organization to make use of customer's advisory directed from brand communities, would address the points Cova and Salle (2008) underlined as above: as the service evaluates to a better configured and satisfactory level for customers, the effect of diffusion of the newly developed version of the service in the brand community would be easier and faster in response to the support of identified contributors in that community. The same issue of consumer networks and their central role in value creation and exchange was also noted by Lusch and Vargo (2006b, p.285) as: "service dominant logic views marketing as social and economic process, in which interaction is central. It embraces the idea that value creation is a process of integrating and transforming resources, which requires interaction and implies networks". With this perspective, SDLM approach and brand communities are intersecting in the co-creation of value by evaluation of services.

Furthermore, non-geographical nature (Muniz and O'Guinn, 2001) of brand communities both support the evaluation of services in different contexts and foster the diffusion of new services in discrete locations, simultaneously. The adoption behavior of brand communities also researched by Thompson and Sinha (2008) recently and the findings were supporting the idea of the increase in the likelihood of adopting a new product from preferred brand as well as the decrease in the opposing brands.

Finally, members of brand community are valuable source of innovation as they have extensive product knowledge and engage in product related discussions in solving problems and generating new product ideas more often than other customers. Making use of customer's advisory for brand communities would be more beneficial for any organization to evaluate their services and innovate new ones out of ideas and views of true believers of their brand. This resource is critically important as it has minimal costs for an innovation process and directly related with consumers of service. Regarding the co-creation of value in consumer networks for "Organizational Adaptiveness to Useful Impulses from Customer" in innovative corporate thinking Michel et al. (2008) address innovations through customers. In this research, the findings claim that innovation in design and customer relations were effective in the revised research model for the use of customer's advisory in the synthesis of strategic imperatives. In parallel with this, Michel et al. (2008) mentioned that the traditional and attribute-based view of innovation should be replaced with more radical SDLM perspective in order to use customers' value co-creation roles in innovation. Lusch and Vargo (2007) extend their views on the role of SDLM in competitive markets with special emphasis on knowledge, collaboration and "sustainable competitive advantage" (p.9) in relation to the proper use of information technologies.

In this perspective, responsiveness and empathy of organization to capture and make use of customer's advisory is blended with technology focus. A revised model for the organizations to make use of customer's advisory is presented below in Figure 4.1.

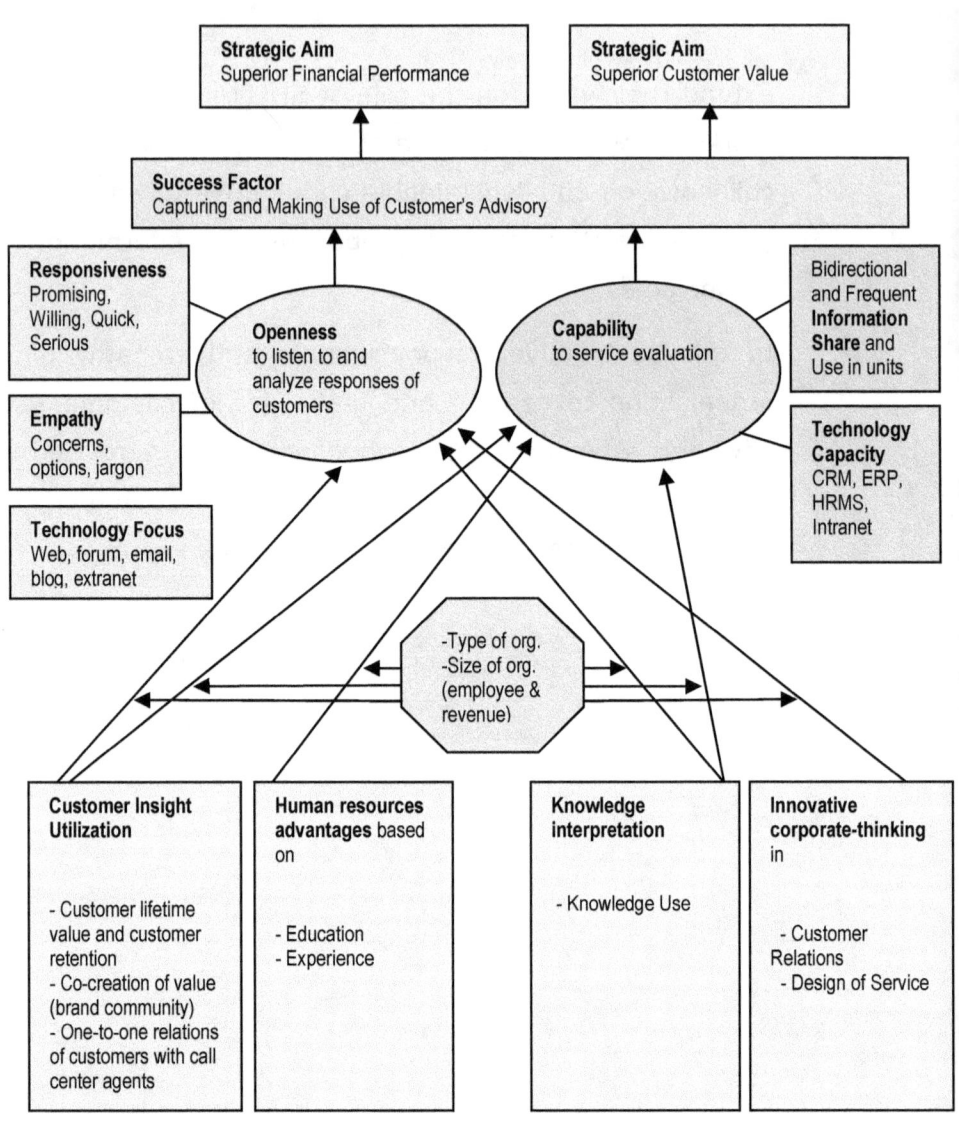

Figure 4.1 Model for Making Use of Customer's Advisory

5   CONCLUSION

Realization of strategic imperatives such as superior customer value and superior financial performance requires a good understanding of organizational development, services development and customer development. Among these aspects, customer development is under the spots of rapid changes. The challenge for organizations is merely a result of technological advancements which empower customer to be more questioning, responsive and more communicative. As Ridderstrale and Nordström (2000, p.102) mentioned: "...The Web enables total transparency. People with access to relevant information are beginning to challenge any type of authority. The stupid, loyal and humble customer, employee, patient or citizen is dead", and this study concluded, Internet and comprehensive organizational web sites are bringing out opportunities for organizations beyond just having conversations with customers, listening to their comments about services offered, collection of their feedbacks about fulfillment of the service, and even how to improve the service to reach a superior customer value.

As a matter of fact, "customer's advisory" contains unconditionally provided cues from customers to revolutionize or evaluate existing products and services. It also opens the door to new product ideas. As innovativeness is a critical key to remain in the competition for globalized markets, this opportunity is unmistakable for organizations. For this reason, the use of customer's advisory requires both organizational responsiveness and empathy to understand customer responses, and capability to turn that information into knowledge for evaluation of services.

Collection of advisory from customers and turning its information to organizational wisdom is depending on several factors.

The first one is the openness of the organization to listen to customer. Responsiveness, empathy and technological focus are the three major components of openness. The results of the research explained that promising attitude, quick response and seriousness were significantly affecting responsiveness component, organizational empathy was stated by taking concerns of customer completely into consideration, explanation of proper technical jargon about service and providing all possible options to customer.

A fully informative and interactive web site, e-mailing, social network blogging, e-forums, extranets are significantly effective marketing technology tools in technology focus of organization to make use of customer's advisory.

The second one is the capability of service evaluation in the organization and better frequency and bilateral sharing information among departments and tools of technology capability were found affective in the evaluation of services for better and innovative. In Turkey, organizations defined the requirements for contributing the synthesis of customer advisory as effective responsiveness, conquered empathy, having interactive marketing communication through technology focus and capability, and frequent information flow between the veins of organization.

Responsiveness of the organization was found dependent to its willingness, promising attitude, quickness and seriousness. Willingness, promising attitude, quickness and seriousness were defined by Parasuraman et al. (1988, 1991b) in SERVQUAL measure. From service quality point of view, responsiveness of the organization was a critical aspect of this measure. It was stated by Parasuraman et al. (1988) as "willingness to help customers and provide prompt service". Making use of customer's advisory requires a good understanding and therefore openness to impulses from customers.

Significance in responsiveness construct represents that an organization is willing and capable to capture better signals and impulses from customer as long as it holds promising attitude, quick response and seriousness in the way they contact with their customers. An organization shows its promising attitude in several ways such as: handling customer demands and complaints in timely manner with a solution, keeping aligned with messages from brand like slogans and mottos, providing the best possible effort to support customer's actions, and communicating effectively with customers not only limited to salvation of any problematic issue but at all times. More or less all of these ways are secured by seriousness of the personnel and management of the organization, to meet a successful result and better relationship. Thus, serious, quick and promising organizational behavior also matters in trust and commitment issues where customer feels much confident with the brand to consume and to contribute its evaluation as well.

Empathy in the organizational behavior was found important and based on understanding concerns of customers well enough and providing explanations of options accurately to the customers. Understanding concerns of customer implies that organization and its employees are putting themselves into customer's shoes when following the feedback, response and advisory of the customer in order to make it real or solved. In parallel with responsiveness, explanation of options to customer supports the informative approach with possible actions available to take when the feedback or complaint is taken. Summing up these two items, an organization which truly makes empathy with its customers through anticipation of concerns and providing alternatives with responsiveness, gains the openness to listen to customer where making use of customer's advisory could happen. Also noted in the results, empathy was found affected positively by hierarchical structure of the organization and negatively by competitive environment, significantly. Thus, as the organization has flatter hierarchy it get more possible to make explanations of options to customers more easily, and, as the organization is in higher competition it puts itself more to customers side to understand their concerns better for making them happier.

Technology focus of the organization was the third important factor, following responsiveness and empathy, for openness in the organization to capture customer advisory. Having a well configured web site and direct marketing communication technology were found significant to make use of customer's advisory. Today, web sites of the organization is a key aptitude to get the impression from what that organization is involved with, contributing to, servicing and how it is formed of. According to this research one of the critical items for any organization is a comprehensive web site that would enable interaction with customer through e-mailing and social networking. As a result of this interactivity, it was found significant that capturing and making use of customer's advisory for the evaluation of services is possible. Moreover, technology focus of the organization was also found significantly affected positively by size of the organization and business orientation.

Service evaluation capability of the organization was found dependent to bilateral information sharing frequency between marketing and engineering units and technological capacity to make evaluation. This explained that the more often information shared among the departments of collecting it from customers and developing the services with proper CRM, HRMS, ERP and Intranet systems installed, the better service evaluation capability was exposed.

Customer lifetime valuation and customer retention, co-creation of value with customers and brand community, and one-to-one relations with customers directly through call center agents were found significantly related with core concept. The utilization of customer insight through these factors was affective for using customer's advisory in evaluation of services.

Increasing customer lifetime value, seeking more customer retention, ability to co-create value with customer not only proposition of value to customer, and one-to-one relationship bonding through agents were affective customer insight utilization components in anticipation of customer's advisory.

Innovative corporate-thinking was found important and significant in making use of customer's advisory through its influentions in customer relations and designing better products and services. Innovations in design of services and innovations in building better relationships with customers were affective on better use of the customer's advisory in service evaluation.

Human resources were significantly important for any organization to make use of customer's advisory. If an organization has better experienced and educated personnel it gains better understanding of customer's advisory. Finally, knowledge interpretation capability of the organization is one of the most important and critical ability to make use of customer's advisory.

114

A good understanding of results driven out from the synthesis of customer's advisory supports customer-oriented organizations to step ahead from the crowd. This research also provides specific model for the sector in which any organization has been actively in competition.

Compromising the results from this research, academia and business gained appreciation of the opportunity to be collectively integrated with target market's need assessments, apply a holistic perspective with the network focus and many-to-many approach in marketing, and also enable higher level anticipation of dynamics in consumer behavior.

By this way, this model stresses the importance of customer's advisory for organizations to gain insights and evaluate their services, and in return to remain competitive and provides guidelines for the understanding of making use of customer's advisory through marketing technology tools for the synthesis of strategic imperatives: superior financial performance and superior customer value.

REFERENCES

Aaker, David (1998). *Strategic Market Management*, New York: USA, Wiley and Sons.

Afiouni, Fida (2007), "Human Resource Management and Knowledge Management: A Road Map Toward Improving Organizational Performance". Journal of American Academy of Business, Cambridge, 11, 2, pp. 124-132.

Allio, Robert J (2003), "Russell L. Ackoff, iconoclastic management authority, advocates a systematic approach to innovation", Strategy and Leadership, 31, 3, pg. 19.

Ang, Lawrence and Francis Buttle (2006), "Managing For Successful Customer Acquisition: An Exploration", Journal of Marketing Management, 22, 3, pg. 295.

Aramburu, Nekane and Josune Sáenz (2007), "Promoting people-focused knowledge management: the case of IDOM", Journal of Knowledge Management, 11, 4, pg. 72.

Aydın, Mehmet N., Mustafa Ö. Güngör and Sevil Özer (2000), "Eliminating Redundancies in Cascaded Supply Chains and Its Organizational Implications", Academia / Industry Working Conference on Research Challenges,SUNY/Buffalo-New York, USA.

Babakuş, Emin and Gregory W. Boller (1992), "An Empirical Assessment of the SERVQUAL Scale", Journal of Business Research, 24, 3, pg. 253.

Bartels, Robert (1965), "Marketing Technology, Tasks, and Relationships", Journal of Marketing, 29, 1, pg. 45.

Beaujean, Marc, Jonathan Davidson and Stacey Madge (2006), "The 'moment of truth' in customer service", McKinsey Quarterly, 1, p.63.

Berkhout, A. J. Guus and Patrick van der Duin (2006), "New ways of innovation: an application of the Cyclical Innovation Model to mobile telecom industry" , Delft Innovation System Papers, 3, pp 1-23.

Berry, Leonard L. (1983). *Relationship Marketing*, Chicago: USA, American Marketing Association.

Berry, Leonard L. and A. Parasuraman (1997), "Listening to the Customer – The Concept of Service-Quality Information System", Sloan Management Review, 38, 3, pp. 65-78.

Berry, Leonard L. and Neeli Bendapudi (2003), "Clueing In Customers", Harvard Business Review, 81, 2, pg. 126.

Berthon, Pierre, Morris B. Holbrook, James M. Hulbert and Leyland F. Pitt (2007), "Viewing Brands in Multiple Dimensions", Sloan Management Review, 48, 2, pg 37.

Bettencourt, Lance A. and Anthony W. Ulwick (2008), "The Customer-Centered Innovation Map" , Harvard Business Review, 86, 5, pp 109-118.

Bickart, Barbara and Robert M. Schindler (2001), "Internet Forums as Influential Sources of Consumer Information", Journal of Interactive Marketing, 15, 3, pg. 31.

Bonabeau, Eric (2002), "Agent-based modeling: Methods and techniques for simulating human systems", Proceedings of the National Academy of Sciences, 99, 3, pg. 7280.

Bonabeau, Eric, Neil Bodick and Robert W. Armstrong (2008), "A More Rational Approach to New-Product Development", Harvard Business Review, 86, 3, pp 96-105.

Borak, Eser H. (1995), "Development of Consumer Consciousness in Turkey -Policy of Consumer Protection Through Reformation", Boğaziçi University Review of Social Economic and Administrative Studies Journal, 9, 2, pp. 123-151.

117

Bowman, Douglas and Das Narayandas, (2004), "Linking Customer Management Effort to Customer Profitability in Business Markets", Journal of Marketing Research, 41, 4, pg. 433.

Buttle, Francis (1996), "SERVQUAL: Review, critique, research agenda", European Journal of Marketing, 30, 1, pg. 8.

Bygdås, Arne Lindseth, Emil Røyrvik and Bjørn Gjerde (2004), "Integrative visualisation and knowledge-enabled value creation: An activity-based approach to intellectual capital", Journal of Intellectual Capital, 5, 4, pg. 540.

Carlucci, Daniela and Giovanni Schiuma (2006), "Knowledge asset value spiral: linking knowledge assets to company's performance", Knowledge and Process Management, 13, 1, pg. 35.

Carman, James M. (1990), "Consumer Perceptions Of Service Quality: An Assessment Of the SERVQUAL Dimensions", Journal of Retailing, 66, 1, pg. 33.

Chenet, Pierre, Caroline Tynan and Arthur Money (1999), "Service performance gap: Re-evaluation and redevelopment", Journal of Business Research, 46, 2, pg. 133.

Christensen, L. Thoger, Simon Torp and A. Fuat Fırat (2005), "Integrated marketing communication and postmodernity: an odd couple ?", Corporate Communications, 10, 2, pp 156.

Clauser, Robert C. (2001),"Offline Rules, Online Tools" Journal of Brand Management, 8, 6, pp. 270-287.

Cooper, Lee G. (2000), "Strategic Marketing Planning for Radically New Products", Journal of Marketing, January, pg. 1.

Cova, Bernard and Robert Salle (2008), "Marketing solutions in accordance with the S-D logic: Co-creating value with customer network actors", Industrial Marketing Management, 37, 3, pg. 270.

Cram, Tony (2001). *Customers That Count*, New Jersey: USA, Prentice Hall.

Cronin, J. Joseph, and Steven A. Taylor (1994), "SERVPERF versus SERVQUAL; Reconciling performance-based abd Perceptions-Minus Expectations Mersurament of Service Quality", Journal of Marketing, 58, 1, pg. 125.

Davenport, Thomas H. and Jeanne G. Harris (2007). *Competing on Analytics: The New Science of Winning*, Boston: USA, Harvard Business School Press.

Day, George S. (1999). *The Market Driven Organization*, New York: USA, Free Press.

Dellarocas, Chrysanthos (2006), "Strategic Manipulation of Internet Opinion Forums: Implications for Consumers and Firms", Management Science, 25, 10, pg. 1577.

Dick, Alan S. and Kunal Basu (1994), "Customer loyalty: toward an integrated framework", Journal of the Academy of Marketing Science, 22, 2, pp. 99-113.

Dwyer, F. Robert (1997),"Customer lifetime valuation to support marketing decision making",Journal of Direct Marketing,11,4,pg.6.

Dwyer, Paul (2007), "Measuring the value of electronic word of mouth and its impact in consumer communities", Journal of Interactive Marketing, 21, 2, pg. 63.

Fırat, A. Fuat, Nikhilesh Dholakia, and Alladi Venkatesh (1995), "Marketing in a postmodern world", European Journal of Marketing, 29, 1, pg. 40.

Fisher, Robert J., Elliot Maltz and Bernard J. Jaworski (1997), "Enhancing communication between marketing and engineering: the moderating role of functional identification", Journal of Marketing, 61, 3, pg. 54.

Fisk, Peter (2006). *Marketing Genius*, West Sussex: England, Capstone Publishing Limited.

119

Frey, Robert S. (2001), "Knowledge management, proposal development, and small businesses", The Journal of Management Development, 20, 1, pg. 38.

Gale, Bradley T. (1994). *Managing Customer Value*, New York: USA, Free Press.

Gibson, Rowan (1996). *Rethinking The Future: Rethinking Business, Principles, Competition, Control and Complexity, Leadership, Markets and the World*, London: UK , N. Brealey Publishing Ltd..

Gobé, Marc. (2002). *Citizen Brand*, New York: USA, Allworth Press.

Gopal, Ram D., Bhavik Pathak, Arvind K. Tripathi and Fang Yin (2006), "From Fatwallet to Ebay: An Investigation of Online Deal-Forums and Sales Promotion", Journal of Retailing, 82, 2, pg. 155.

Griffith, David A., Stephanie M. Noble and Qimei Chen (2006), "The performance implications of entrepreneurial proclivity: A dynamic capabilities approach", Journal of Retailing, 82, 1, pg. 51.

Grönroos, Christian (2004), "The relationship marketing process: communication, interaction, dialogue, value", Journal of Business and Industrial Marketing, 19, 2, pg.99.

Grönroos, Christian (2008),"Service logic revisited:who creates value? And who co-creates?",European Business Rev.,20,4, pg.298.

Gummesson, Evert (2002), "Practical value of adequate marketing management theory",European Journal of Marketing, 36, 3, pg. 325.

Gupta, Sunil and Donald R. Lehmann (2005). *Managing Customers As Investments*, Philadelphia: USA, Wharton School Publishing.

Güngör, M. Özgür and Kaan Aktoluğ (2007), "Understanding the changes in Supply Chain Management: Extensions with a Strategic Marketing Perspective", 3rd International Conference on Economics and Management of Networks, Erasmus University Rotterdam, Netherlands.

Hammer, Michael and James Champy (1993). *Reengineering The Corporation*, New York: USA, HarperCollins Publishers.

Harrison-Walker, L. Jean (2001), "E-Complaining: A Content Analysis of an Internet Complaint Forum", Journal of Services Marketing, 15, 4/5, pg. 397.

Hoch, Stephen J. and John Deighton (1989), "Managing What Consumers Learn From Experience", Journal of Marketing,53,2, p. 1.

Holsapple, Clyde W. (2005), "The inseparability of modern knowledge management and computer-based technology", Journal of Knowledge Management, 9, 1, pg. 42.

Huber, Frank, Andreas Herrmann and Robert E. Morgan (2001), "Gaining competitive advantage through customer value oriented management", The Journal of Consumer Marketing, 18, 1, pg. 41.

Hunt, Shelby D. (1997), "Resource-advantage theory: An evolutionary theory of competitive firm behavior?", Journal of Economic Issues, 31, 1, pg. 59

Hunt, Shelby D. and Robert M. Morgan (1997), "Resource-advantage Theory: A snake swallowing its tail or a general theory of competition?" Journal of Marketing, 61, pg 74.

Hunt, Shelby D. and Dennis B. Arnett (2003), "Resource-advantage theory and embeddedness: Explaining R-A theory's explanatory success", Journal of Marketing theory and Practice, 11, 1, pg 1.

Jacobson, Robert and David A. Aaker (1987), "The Strategic Role of Product Quality", Journal of Marketing, 51, 4, pg. 31.

Jain, Dipak and Siddartha S. Singh (2002), "Customer Lifetime Value Research in Marketing: A Review and Future Directions", Journal of Interactive Marketing, 16, 2, pg. 34.

Johnson, Michael D. and Anders Gustafsson (2000). *Improving Customer Satisfaction, Loyalty, and Profit*, San Francisco: USA, Jossey-Bass.

121

Kalaignanam, Kartik, Tarun Kushwaha, and Rejan P. Varadarajan (2008), "Marketing operations efficiency and the Internet: An organizing framework", Journal of Business Research, 61, 4, pg. 300

Katz, Elihu and Paul F. Lazarsfeld (1955). *Personal Influence: The Part Played By People in the Flow of Mass Communications*, New York: USA, Free Press.

Kitchen, Philip J. and Don E. Schultz (2003), "Integrated corporate and product brand communication", Advances in Competitiveness Research, 11, pg. 66.

Kohli, Ajay K. and Bernard J. Jaworski (1990), "Market orientation: the construct, research propositions, and managerial implications", Journal of Marketing, 54, 2, pg. 1.

Koslowsky, Sam (2001), "The marketing cube", Journal of Financial Services Marketing, 6, 2, pg. 164.

Lemon Katherine N., Roland T. Rust and Valerie A. Zeithaml (2001), "What drivers customer equity",Marketing Management,10,1,pg. 20.

Levitt, Barbara and James G. March (1988), "Organizational Learning", Annual Review of Sociology, 14, pg. 319.

Little, John D.C (1979), "Decision Support Systems for Marketing Managers", Journal of Marketing, 43, 3, pg. 9.

Luo, Xueming (2007), "Consumer Negative Voice and Firm-Idiosyncratic Stock Returns", Journal of Marketing, 71, 3, pg. 75.

Lusch, Robert F. and Stephen L. Vargo (2004), "Evolving to a New Dominant Logic for Marketing",Journal of Marketing, 68, 1. pp. 1-17.

Lusch, Robert F. and Stephen L Vargo (2006a). *The Service-Dominant Logic of Marketing: Dialog, Debate, and Directions*, New York: USA, M.E.Sharpe.

Lusch, Robert F. and Stephen L Vargo (2006b). "Service-dominant logic:reactions, reflections and refinements", Marketing Theory, 6, 3, pp. 281-288.

Lusch, Robert F., Stephen L. Vargo, and Matthew O'Brien (2007), "Competing through service: Insights from service-dominant logic", Journal of Retailing, 83, 1, pp. 5-18.

Malthouse, Edward C. and Robert C. Blattberg (2004), "Can we predict customer lifetime value?". Journal of Interactive Marketing. 19, 1 pg. 2.

Maltz, Elliot and Ajay K. Kohli (1996), "Market Intelligence Dissemination Across Functional Boundaries," Journal of Marketing Research, 33, pp 47-61.

Marsden, James R. (2008), "The Internet and DSS: massive, real-time data availability is changing the DSS landscape", Information Systems and eBusiness Management, 6, 2, pg. 193.

Mascarenhas, Oswald A., Ram Kesavan, Michael Bernacchi (2004), "Customer value-chain involvement for co-creating customer delight", The Journal of Consumer Marketing, 21, 7, pg. 486.

Massey Graham R. and Elias Kyriazis (2007). "Interpersonal Trust between Marketing and R&D during new product development projects," European Journal of Marketing, 9/10, pp. 1146-1172.

Mayzlin, Dina (2006), "Promotional Chat on the Internet", Marketing Science, 25, 2, pg. 155.

Menon, Anil and Rajan Varadarajan (1992). "A Model of Marketing Knowledge Use Within Firms," Journal of Marketing, 56, pp 53-7 1.

Merisavo, Marko and Mika Raulas (2004), "The Impact of E-Mail Marketing on Brand Loyalty", Journal of Product and Brand Management, 13, 7, pg. 498.

Michel, Stefan, Stephen W Brown, Andrew S Gallan (2008), "Service-Logic Innovations: How to Innovate Customers, Not Products", California Management Review, 50, 3, pg. 49.

Morgan, Robert M, and Shelby D. Hunt (1994), "Relationship-Based Competitive Advantage: The Role of Relationship Marketing in Marketing Strategy", Journal of Business Research, 46, 3, pg. 281.

Muniz, Albert M. and Thomas C. O'Guinn (2001). "Brand Community". Journal of Consumer Research, 27, 4. pg. 412

Nambisan, Satish and Priya Nambisan (2008). "How to Profit from a Better 'Virtual Customer Environment'", Sloan Management Review, 49, 3, pp. 53-61.

Ozuem, Wilson, Kerry E. Howell, and Geoff Lancaster (2008), "Communicating in the new interactive marketspace", European Journal of Marketing, 42, 9/10, pg. 1059

Parasuraman, A, Valerie A. Zeithaml and Leonard L. Berry (1985), "A Conceptual Model of Service Quality and its Implications for Future Research", Journal of Marketing, 49, 1, pp.41-50.

Parasuraman, A, Valerie A. Zeithaml and Leonard L. Berry (1988), "SERVQUAL: A multiple-item scale for measuring consumer perceptions of service quality", Journal of Retailing, 64, 1, pp.12-40.

Parasuraman, A., Leonard L. Berry and Valerie A. Zeithaml (1991a), "Understanding Customer Expectations of Service", Sloan Management Review, 32, 3, pg. 39.

Parasuraman, A, Valerie A. Zeithaml and Leonard L. Berry (1991b), "Refinement and reassessment of the SERVQUAL scale", Journal of Retailing, 67, 4, pp.420-450.

Parasuraman, A., Valerie A. Zeithaml and Leonard L. Berry (1994), "Resassesment of expectations as a comparison standard in measuring Service Quality: Implications for Future Reseach", Journal of Marketing, 55, 1, pp.111-124.

Parasuraman, A. (2000a). "Technology readiness index (TRI): A multiple-item scale to measure readiness to embrace new technologies", Journal of Service Research, 2, 4, pp. 307-320.

Parasuraman, A. and Dhruv Grewal (2000b). "The impact of Technology on the Quality-Value-Loyalty Chain: A Research Agenda", Academy of Marketing Science Journal, 28, 1, pg. 168.

Payne, Adrian and Pennie Frow (2005). "A strategic framework for CRM",Journal of Marketing,69,pg. 167.

Pfeifer, Phillip E., Mark E. Haskins and Robert M. Conroy (2005). "Customer Lifetime Value, Customer Profitability, and the Treatment of Acquisition Spending",Journal of Managerial Issues, 17, 1, pg. 11.

Pietsch Gotthart (2007). "Human Capital Measurement, Ambiguity, and Opportunism: Actors between Menace and Opportunity", Zeitschrift für Personalforschung, 21, 3, pg. 252.

Porter, Michael E. (1985). *Competitive Advantage*, New York: USA, Free Press.

Porter, Michael E. (2008), "The five competitive forces that shape strategy", Harvard Business Review, 86, 1, pg. 1.

Proctor, Robert (1991). *Value-Free Science?: Purity and Power in Modern Knowledge*, Boston:USA, Harvard College.

Reichheld, Frederick F. (1996). *The Loyalty Effect*, Boston: USA, Harvard Business School Press.

Ridderstrale Jonas and Kjell Nordström (2000). *Funky Business: Talent Makes Capital Dance*, Stockholm: Sweden, BookHouse Publishing AB.

Ries Al, and Jack Trout (1981). *Positioning*, New York: USA, Mc-Graw-Hill.

Roos, G, Lisa Fernstrom, S Pike (2004). "Human resource management and business performance measurement". Mesuring Business Excellence, 8, 1, pp. 28-38.

Rosen, Emanuel (2000). *The Anatomy of Buzz: How to Create Word-of-Mouth Marketing*, New York: USA, Currency-Double Day of Random House.

Ruekert, Robert W (1992), "Developing a Market Orientation: An Organizational Strategy Perspective", International Journal of Research in Marketing, 9, 3, pg. 225.

Ruyter, Ko de and Martin Wetzels (1998), "Customer equity considerations in service recovery: a cross-industry perspective", Int'l Journal of Service Industry Management, 11, 1, pg. 91.

Schiemann William A. (2006). "People Equity: A New Paradigm for Measuring and Managing Human Capital". Human Rsource Planning, 29, 1, pp. 34-45.

Senge, Peter (1990). *The Fifth Discipline: The Art and Practice of the Learning Organization*, New York: USA, Random House.

Shapiro, Benson P. (1988), "What the Hell Is Market Oriented?", Harvard Business Review, 66, pg.119

Sheth Jagdish N. and Atul Parvatiyar (1995). "The Evolution of Relationship Marketing", International Business Review, 4, pg. 397.

Silvie, R. Albert and Ronald C. Fetzer (2005), "Smart community networks: self-directed team effectiveness in action", Team Performance Management, 11, 5/6, pp. 144-156.

Simmons, Geoff (2008), "Marketing to postmodern consumers: introducing the internet chameleon", European Journal of Marketing, 42, 3/4, pg. 299.

Slater, Stanley F, and John C. Narver (1994), "Does competitive environment moderate the market orientation-performance relationship?", Journal of Marketing, 58, 1, pg. 46.

Smith, J Brock, and Mark Colgate (2007), "Customer Value Creation: A Practical Framework", Journal of Marketing Theory and Practice, 15, 1, pp. 7-25.

Speier, Cheri and Viswanath Venkatesh (2002), "The hidden minefields in the adoption of sales force automation technologies", Journal of Marketing, 66, 3, pp. 98-111.

Stephens, Marilyn (1996), "Global marketing challenges and opportunities for manufacturers' representatives", Marketing Intelligence and Planning, 14, 5, pg. 25.

Stuart, Spencer (2005), "Mastering CRM", A Report by American Marketing Association, pp. 37-51. (www.marketingpower.com)

Svoboda, Robert S. (2006), "Value in Use vs. Value in Exchange", Valuation Strategies, 9, 3, pg.26.

Tek Ö. Baybars (2006). *Pazarlamada Değer Yaratmak (Value Creation in Marketing)*, Istanbul: Turkey, Hayat Yayıncılık.

Thelwall, Mike (2008), "No place for news in social network web sites?", Online Information Review, 32, 6, pg. 726.

Thomas, Jacquelyn, Werner Reinartz and V. Kumar (2004), "Getting the most out of all your customers". Harvard Business Review, 82, 7, pg.117.

Thompson, Scott A and Rajiv K Sinha (2008), "Brand Communities and New Product Adoption:The Influence and Limits of Oppositional Loyalty", Journal of Marketing, 72, 6, pg. 65.

Tiwana, Amrit (2001). *The Essential Guide to Knowledge Management*, New Jersey: USA, Prentice Hall.

Tseng, Fan-Chen, Ching-I Teng, and David M. Chiang (2007), "Delivering Superior Customer Perceived Value in the Context of Network Effects", Int'l Journal of E-Business Research, 3, 1, pg. 41.

Uysal, Gurhan (2009), "Human Resource Management in the US, Europe and Asia: Differences and Characteristics", Journal of American Academy of Business, Cambridge, 14, 2, p. 112.

Van Bruggen, Gerrit H., Ale Smidts and Berend Wierenga (2001), "The powerful triangle of marketing data, managerial judgement, and marketing management support systems", European Journal of Marketing, 35, 7, pp.796-814.

Van Dolen, Willemijn M., Pratibha A. Dabholkar and Ko de Ruyter (2007), "Satisfaction with Online Commercial Group Chat: The Influence of Perceived Technology Attributes, Chat Group Characteristics, and Advisor Communication Style", Journal of Retailing, 83, 3, pg. 339.

Voss, Glenn B. and Zannie Giraud Voss (2008), "Competitive Density and the Customer Acquisition-Retention Trade-Off", Journal of Marketing, 72, 6, pg.3.

Walker, Orville C. and Robert W. Ruekert (1987), "Marketing's Role in the Implementation of Business Strategies: A Critical Review and Conceptual Framework". Journal of Marketing, pg. 15.

Weinstein, Art and William C. Johnson (1999). *Designing and Delivering Superior Customer Value*, Florida: USA, St. Lucie Press.

Whitney, Margaret A. (1989), "Analyzing Corporate Communications Policy Using Ethnographic Methods", IEEE Transactions on Professional Communication, 32, 2, pg. 76.

Wierenga, Berend, Gerrit H. Van Bruggen and Richard Staelin (1999), "The success of marketing management support systems". Marketing Science, 18, 3, pp.196-207.

Zaltman, Gerald (2003). *How Customers Think*, Boston: USA, Harvard Business School Press.

Zeithaml, Valerie A., Leonard L. Berry and A. Parasuraman (1996), "The Behavioral Consequences of Service Quality", Journal of Marketing, 60, 2, pg. 31.